Analysing the Errors and Exposing the Real Agenda of Pierre Teilhard de Chardin S.J.

Selected Works of Frits Albers

(Volume 1)

Frits Albers

Edited and with a Foreword by

Frank Calneggia

En Route Books and Media, LLC

Saint Louis, MO

USA

⊛ENROUTE
Make the time

En Route Books and Media, LLC

5705 Rhodes Avenue

St. Louis, MO 63109

Cover credit: Sebastian Mahfood using Michelangelo's Sistine Chapel image (1508-1512) of God creating Adam.

Copyright © 2024 Michael P. Albers

ISBN-13: 979-8-88870-179-9

Library of Congress Control Number: 2024939121

Dedication

One line held out (against Modernism) headed by the Holy Father (Pope Paul VI). We cannot be surprised that this line consists of Catholics who, steeped in the Traditions of their own country, with a singular devotion to Our Lady of Fatima and with the so necessary 'discipline of the mind', have rejected Teilhardism and its false interpretations of Vatican II; and who are now in a privileged position of 'undoing the knot of Eve of our time', and of passing the Catholic Church wholly intact to the next generation. To these heroes and heroines, youthful and old, I devote my entire opus.

On the Feast Day of Our Lady of Fatima,
October 13, 1979.

Quotations

"That our Catholic faith, without which it is impossible to please God, may, errors being purged away, continue in its own perfect and spotless integrity, and that the Christian people may not be carried about with every wind of doctrine; whereas that old serpent, the perpetual enemy of mankind, amongst the very many evils with which the Church of God is in these our times troubled, has also stirred up not only new, but even old, dissensions touching original sin, and the remedy thereof; the sacred and holy, ecumenical and general Synod of Trent, - lawfully assembled in the Holy Ghost, the three same legates of the Apostolic See presiding therein, - wishing now to come to the reclaiming of the erring, and the confirming of the wavering, - following the testimonies of the sacred Scriptures, of the holy Fathers, of the most approved councils, and the judgment and consent of the Church itself, ordains, confesses, and declares these things touching the said original sin:

1. If any one does not confess that the first man, Adam, when he had transgressed the commandment of God in Paradise, immediately lost the holiness and justice wherein he had been constituted; and that he incurred, through the offence of that prevarication, the wrath and indignation of God, and consequently death, with which God had previously threatened him, and, together with death, captivity under his power who thenceforth had the empire of death, that is to say, the devil, and that the entire Adam, through that offence of prevarication, was changed, in body and soul, for the worse; let him be anathema.

Selected Works of Frits Albers on Pierre Teilhard de Chardin, S.J.

"2. If any one asserts, that the prevarication of Adam injured himself alone, and not his posterity; and that the holiness and justice, received of God, which he lost, he lost for himself alone, and not for us also; or that he, being defiled by the sin of disobedience, has only transfused death, and pains of the body, into the whole human race, but not sin also, which is the death of the soul; let him be anathema: - whereas he contradicts the apostle who says; "By one man sin entered into the world, and by sin death, and so death passed upon all men, in whom all have sinned." (Rom 5, 12) ....

Canons and Decrees of the Council of Trent

Fifth Session, 17 June 1646.

Decree Concerning Original Sin.

"(14) Hence, too, that meaning of the sacred dogmas is ever to be maintained which has once been declared by Holy mother Church, and there must never be any abandonment of this sense under the pretext or in the name of a more profound understanding.

May understanding, knowledge and wisdom increase as ages and centuries roll along, and greatly and vigorously flourish, in each and all, in the individual and the whole Church: but this only in its own proper kind, that is to say, in the same doctrine, the same sense, and the same understanding."

Vatican Council I. Session 3: 24 April 1870

Dogmatic Constitution on the Catholic Faith

Chapter 4: "On Faith and Reason"

"37. When, however, there is question of another conjectural opinion, namely polygenism, the children of the Church by no means enjoy such liberty. For the faithful cannot embrace that opinion which maintains that either after Adam there existed on this earth true men who did not take their origin through natural generation from him as from the first parent of all, or that Adam represents a certain number of first parents. Now it is in no way apparent how such an opinion can be reconciled with that which the sources of revealed truth and the documents of the Teaching Authority of the Church propose with regard to original sin, which proceeds from a sin actually committed by an individual Adam and which, through generation, is passed on to all and is in everyone as his own." (Cfr. *Rom.*, V, 12-19; Conc. Trid., sess, V, can. 1-4.)"

Pope Pius XII
Encyclical
Humani Generis
12 August 1950

"4. In making this profession, we are aware of the disquiet which agitates certain modern quarters with regard to the faith. They do not escape the influence of a world being profoundly changed, in which so many certainties are being disputed or discussed. We see even Catholics allowing themselves to be seized by a kind of passion for change and novelty. The Church, most assuredly, has always the duty to carry on the effort to study more deeply and to present, in a manner ever better adapted to successive generations, the unfathomable mysteries of God, rich for all in fruits of salvation. But at the same time the greatest care must be taken, while fulfilling the indispensable duty of research, to do no injury to the teachings of Christian doctrine. For that would be to give, rise, as is unfortunately seen in these days, to disturbance and perplexity in many faithful souls.

16. We believe that in Adam all have sinned, which means that the original offense committed by him caused human nature, common to all men, to fall to a state in which it bears the consequences of that offense, and which is not the state in which it was at first in our first parents—established as they were in holiness and justice, and in which man knew neither evil nor death. It is human nature so fallen, stripped of the grace that clothed it, injured in its own natural powers and subjected to the dominion of death, that is transmitted to all men, and it is in this sense that every man is born in sin. We therefore hold, with the Council of Trent, that original sin is transmitted with human nature, "not by imitation, but by propagation" and that it is thus "proper to everyone." (Cf. Dz.-Sch. 1513.)"

Pope Paul VI.
Apostolic Letter in the Form of *Motu Proprio*
Solemni Hac Liturgia
(Credo of the People of God)
June 30, 1968

Table of Contents

Foreword

by Frank Calneggia

The more senior orthodox Catholics who read this selection of the works of Frits Albers will well remember the confusion and disappointment that descended upon them not so long after the Second Vatican Council had concluded - confusion and disappointment engendered by the strange things they heard preached from the pulpit; by the strange things they read in Catholic newspapers; by the strange things religious and lay experts taught them in a host of seminars, retreats, encounter groups and such like; but worst of all, by the *volte face* their children were subjected to in the name of Catholic Education. This swarm of aberrations and contradictions of age-old Catholic teaching, it was explained to them, were the necessary reforms demanded by the recently concluded Second Vatican Council.

A general reaction amongst Catholics to these repeated assertions placed many of them (unenviably) at either one of two opposing poles. One group, who might be styled the *avant-garde* or progressive group (modernists), reacted with triumph: 'thank God they have changed the Church!'. The other group, who took to themselves the name 'Traditionalists', reacted in a dour manner: 'Oh no, they have changed the Church!'. This reaction was common to both groups because in each instance it invoked the *post hoc ergo propter hoc* fallacy: after Vatican II 'the Church has fundamentally changed' therefore it was because of Vatican II that 'the

Church has fundamentally changed'. In contradiction of this falla-cy St Paul assures us that "Jesus Christ is the same yesterday, and today, and forever" (Heb 13:8), and that Jesus Christ is the Head of His Body which is the Church. (Col 1:18, Eph 1:22-23).

The right reaction to dubious explanations of the teaching of Vatican II is straightforward enough: compare the actual teaching of Vatican II <u>and</u> the pre-conciliar Church to the aberrations and contradictions claimed to have been sanctioned by the Council.

One of the first in Australia to make such a serious study and comparison was Frits Albers. Not only did he accurately note the contradictions of Catholic Teaching that were claimed to have been taught by Vatican II, he also identified very early the philoso-phy behind these contradictions and errors. He realised it was the same philosophy he had been taught in the 1940's by the Jesuits at Nijmegen (Holland) in the name of St Thomas Aquinas, but which in reality was the systematic Modernism of Pierre Teilhard de Chardin S.J. Thus, in the early 1970's he began writing articles and books to expose the philosophical root of the errors and aberra-tions of Teilhard de Chardin and the false ecumenism that was be-ing built upon them. His overriding aim was to defend Catholic Faith, clear thinking and right philosophy rooted in the principles of St Thomas Aquinas. He also wrote some beautiful works on Our Lady.

Frits drew much instruction and inspiration from the teaching of Pope St Pius X. Much to the chagrin of those who, in conse-quence, tried to label and dismiss his writings against Modernism and Teilhardism as the work of a Latin Mass fanatic or tradition-al-ist, he wrote strenuously and effectively to defend Vatican II and the *Novus Ordo Missae* promulgated by Pope Paul VI. Of Pope Paul VI he wrote in one of his early books "he may well be a saint". His love for and defense of Vatican II and the *Novus Ordo* was unshakeable.

Selected for publication in this present volume are four of the principal works of Frits Albers wherein the errors of Pierre Teilhard de Chardin S.J. are exposed and analysed in depth, their impact on critical areas of Catholic life made manifest, and Teilhard's real agenda proved from Teilhard's own words. They are the following books and booklets.

- *Teilhard de Chardin and the Dutch Catechism*;
- *The Hidden Schism*;
- *The 'Theology' of the late Pierre Teilhard de Chardin, S.J.*;
- *Tradition*

For the first of these works, *Teilhard de Chardin and the Dutch Catechism*, the author received, from the *Secretariate of State of the Vatican*, in a letter dated 21st September 1974, "commendation for his theological and philosophical doctrine, which, together with the thanks of the Holy Father, is expressed herewith in the name of His Holiness".

In *Teilhard de Chardin and the Dutch Catechism* the author traces the root error of Teilhard's systematic Modernism to its foundation in three privately circulated papers wherein Teilhard formulated a new philosophy (the 'philosophy of sameness') to do away with the Dogma of Original Sin and to allow him thereby to fuse the supernatural (God) with the natural (Creation). Teilhard wanted to obliterate the real distinction between God and His Creation so that he could assign to God the function of being the soul of an evolving universe. (In dealing with such people one is constantly reminded of the words of Pope St Pius X "audacity is their chief characteristic". *Pascendi*, 1907)

The author then proves by means of a through exposition and analysis of philosophy course texts that Teilhard's 'philosophy of sameness' (sameness of God and His Creation) was already being taught by the Jesuits in their Houses of Study at Louvain and Nijmegen to candidates for the priesthood in the mid to late 1940s, and as the foundation of the Dutch Catechism which the Jesuits subsequently wrote.

Teilhard de Chardin and the Dutch Catechism first appeared in print (1974) in the *Journal of the International Catholic Priests' Association* through the good offices of the then Secretary Rev. Fr. John W. Flanagan S.T.L., D.C.L.

The second of these books, *The Hidden Schism*, first appeared in print (1975) also through the efforts of Fr. Flanagan. The full title of the original publication was *The Hidden Schism or The New Catholicism.*

The author divides this book into two parts. In the first part he presents convincing evidence that the school of Modernism of Loisy and Terrell condemned by Pope St. Pius X was developed into the Systematic Modernism of Teilhard de Chardin condemned by Pope Pius XII. This transition of Modernism into Teilhardism has been written about in many responsible publications and books. What has not been given adequate coverage in such publications and books, though it is of equal if not of more importance, is the preparation employed by the plotters during this transition period so that Teilhardism would be accepted by Catholics after Vatican II as the 'authentic interpretations' of the Council. The author discusses and analyses this insidious preparation in some depth and with much acumen.

The second part of *The Hidden Schism* provides substantial documented evidence of the devastating influence of Teilhardism on Catholic life in a large metropolitan Archdiocese – the Archdiocese of Melbourne, Australia, in which the author lived. The areas of Catholic life the author concentrates upon are Catechetics, Priestly Training and the 1973 International Eucharistic Congress. Though these particular ruptures of Catholic life are now dated their consequences still live on. The exposition and analysis given of them is an important historical record that needs to be understood and learned from regardless of the passage of time.

The third work, *The 'Theology' of the late Pierre Teilhard de Chardin, S.J.*, was printed by the author in 1979. The author presents twenty-four quotes from Teilhard's own writings together with extensive comments upon them to allow readers to come to grips with the essential elements of what has become known as 'Teilhard's theology'. One of those elements uncovered by the author is a 'theological principle' invented by Teilhard that would corrupt the purity and sexual innocence of those who take it to heart as a principle of Teilhard's 'New Catholicism'.

The fourth and final book, *Tradition*, written in 1979, consolidates and builds upon evidence presented and analysed in the three books introduced above. The author reproduces two Addresses of Pope St. John Paul II in which the Holy Father systematically traced the absence of evolution of the human body in Catholic Tradition to its origin in the first chapters of the Book of Genesis.

The author then turns his attention to the documents of Vatican II and shows that they can only be rightly understood when seen and accepted as a continuation of the uninterrupted Tradition (handing on of Revelation) that has always existed in the Church. To give hope and consolation to Catholics who have resisted Teilhardism he brings out some of the beautiful Marian teaching of the Council. He thereafter offers some cogent thoughts on the Council's persistent call to personal holiness and a synthesis in which the relevance and necessity of Vatican II for our times is to be found.

One is hard pressed to find such well researched, perceptive, and penetrating analyses of Teilhard de Chardin and his real agenda anywhere else in modern day Catholic academia as in the four books of Frits Albers introduced above. With the publication of this present volume, it is hoped that this deficiency will start to be overcome so that Truth may shine forth in all its splendour.

Book I

Teilhard de Chardin and The Dutch Catechism

Frits Albers, Ph.B. (1974)

A critical analysis of the philosophies and "Theology" of Teilhard de Chardin and the Dutch Catechism and the interrelation between them.

Preamble

"These false evolutionary notions, with the denial of all that is absolute or fixed or abiding in human experience, have paved the way for a **new philosophy of error**."

"And so it is with these moderns: they go so far, some of them, as to raise serious doubts about our theology and its method. The demand is for their wholesale reform. This, we are told, would make for a more effective spread of Christ's Kingdom all over the world, among men of whatever culture, or whatever religious opinions."

"**The same divine truth**, they tell us, may be expressed on the human side in two different ways, even in **two ways which in a sense contradict one another, and still really mean the same thing**."

"But if reason is to perform this office adequately and **without fear of error**, it must be trained **on the right principles**; it must be steeped in that **sound philosophy** which we have long possessed as an heirloom handed down to us by former ages of Christendom. **These principles upon which it is based have been made, by the teaching authority of the Church, into the touchstone of Divine Revelation**."

"The mind of man when it is engaged in a **sincere** search for truths, **will never light on one which contradicts the truths it has already ascertained**. The Christian will weigh the latest fancy carefully, making sure that he does not lose hold of the truth already in his possession **or contaminate it in any way, with great danger and perhaps great loss to the Faith itself**."

"In view of all this it is not surprising that the Church will have her future priests brought up on a philosophy which derives its method, its system and its basic principles from the **Angelic Doctor** (C.I.C. can 1366, 2). One thing is clearly established by the long experience of the ages: his teaching seems to chime in, by a kind of pre-established harmony, **with Divine Revelation: no surer way to safeguard the First Principles of the Faith.**"

"Philosophical tendencies too **must come under the Church's watchful care, otherwise the whole of Catholic Doctrine may be undermined by false assumptions.**"

Pope Pius XII
Humani Generis
12th August 1950
(emphasis added)

Introduction

Broadly speaking, a philosophy is an outlook on life. It encompasses one's attitude to **truth, morality, life, death, Man and his Mind in relation to God and religion.** In the hands of a professional, this outlook on life becomes a systematic study and research into the various fields mentioned: their reason for existence, their inter relationships and their ultimate finality. There are, of course, as many popular philosophies as there are human beings, but these are all modifications, adaptations and mixtures of only a handful of "systems" of philosophy, or world philosophies.

A philosophy must never be confused with a theology. A theology is much more difficult to popularize. It is by nature systematic and deals essentially with truths as revealed by God, or believed to be revealed by God. This is good to remember, as the *natural* knowledge of God, according to St Paul, rightly belongs to philosophy.

By its very nature a theology presupposes a philosophy: not a vague, popular outlook; but a systematic thought-out science. A good theology is built on a good philosophy, but erroneous philosophy will only support a fallacious theology.

If it does not pay to confuse a philosophy, however good and systematic, with a theology, even more havoc results if theology is made synonymous with faith: the acceptance of a body of articles or dogmas, as held up by the Church to be believed. To be more specific: Catholic theology is a systematic reflection on Revealed Truths, but even Catholic theology **cannot give faith** in these supernatural truths. Theology does not supplant faith nor does it take

5

over its role and function. Nowadays it certainly does not come as a shock to many simple Catholics that some modern theologians appear to have lost altogether their Catholic Faith.

When a person states:

> "God does not exist,
>> so life after death does not exist,
>> so I do not have to worry about the fate of my soul (if I have one),
>> so I can do what I like,
>> subject to man-made laws,
>> which can be changed if enough pressure is put on the Government,
>> so I combine with others
>> to put more pressure on the Government,
>> so it will change the laws to my liking,
>> so I can be freer to do what I please ..."

then one would call such an effort a crude personal philosophy. But, although considered wrong by many people, it would nevertheless by *consistent*, and, in that sense, *logical*. And so this little exercise becomes a system: a system which must be either totally accepted or rejected.

It is in this sense that one of the great scholars on Teilhard de Chardin, Cardinal Journet, wrote in *Nova Et Vetera* (October – December 1962): "Teilhard's synthesis is logical and must be rejected or accepted as a whole." We cannot pick out bits and pieces here and there to our liking.

What is missing of course in the little "system" above is evidence and insight based on evidence. The absence of these will make even the most "logical" system completely erroneous. The first sentence is always the most important because all others are made to follow from it. In reasoning only, it is called a "premise", or "major premise". In a philosophical system it is called a "first principle" or "fundamental principle". It is obvious that it is of the utmost importance for the **whole system** that this **first sentence is true and based on evidence**.

The Catholic Church, conscious of Her Guardianship over matters of Catholic Faith, the *Depositum Fidei*, has absolute and final power over Catholic theology, and so over the underlying philosophy, be it more indirect. Not surprisingly, over two thousand years of tending to the sheep, a distinct Catholic philosophy has developed in which the Catholic Church feels at home. According to the Popes this did not some about "without the promptings of the Holy Ghost".

The Catholic Church has persistently taught the acceptance within the Church of the philosophy of St Thomas Aquinas.

- *Aeterni Patris*, Leo XIII, 4th August 1879, Encyclical,
- *Doctoris Angelici*, St Pius X, 29th June 1914, Motu Proprio;
- *Quod De Fovenda*, Benedict XV, 19th March 1917 Letter to Jesuits.
- *Studiorum Ducem*, Pius XI, 29th June 1923, Encyclical.

These are four major papal works devoted entirely to St Thomas and the study of his works. Furthermore there is the clear directive of the Sacred Congregation of Studies of 7th March 1916, and further extensive directives laid down in another two papal encyclicals.

- *Pascendi Dominici Gregis*, St Pius X, 8th September 1907, and
- *Humani Generis*, Pius XII, 12th August 1950.

In *Pascendi*, for example, the Holy Father clearly talks about attempts being made to introduce into the Catholic Church a *new*, modernistic theology; about the strong links between philosophy and theology, and he points out that the new (bad) theology is required by a new philosophy as follows:

"Lastly, the modernists continuously and openly rebuke the Church on the grounds that she resolutely refuses to submit and accommodate her dogmas to the opinions of philosophy, while they on their side, having for this purpose blotted out the old theology, endeavour to introduce a new theology which shall support the aberrations of philosophers ..."

And in *Humani Generis*, Pope Pius XII clearly states that contamination of the philosophy of St Thomas will lead to serious disorders in Faith itself and even to loss of Faith. (Note that the Pope does not say: the contamination of the theology of St Thomas. No, for disorders in Catholic Faith to become evident it is, according to the Pope, sufficient to have a contamination of the philosophy of St Thomas).

It is against this formidable background of persistent, unerring teaching by the Magisterium of the Catholic Church that the introduction of any new system of philosophy/ theology/Faith must be examined.

Catholics, when dealing with Teilhard, must keep in mind that they are dealing with the works of one of whom it can truly be said that "**the church has resolutely refused to submit and accommodate her dogmas to the opinions of his philosophy**".

Teilhard has no fewer than fourteen known and official interdicts, prohibitions, and outright condemnations against his name and against his works, and at least one Encyclical, *Humani Generis*, easily a record in modern times. Furthermore, the Magisterium has been consistent in the rejection of his books and his theories for over fifty years. If it appears to be impossible, even for a Saint, to introduce into the Church a new system of philosophy acceptable to the Magisterium, what chance has a man got censured so many times? And yet, Teilhard has been hailed by millions as a new St Thomas: he is being seriously studied within the Catholic Church as if he was one. No wonder Catholics are paying dearly for this betrayal and disobedience.

Lastly, in dealing with the *Dutch Catechism*, Catholics, once again, must keep in mind that the book is so erroneous that its publication was forbidden by the Holy See. Extensive alterations in the presentation of Catholic Doctrine were required. These alterations were never made by the authors. The next best thing then was that a Commission of Cardinals made extensive recommendations, which were never incorporated in the original text, as required. They were finally published separately. Without these the *Dutch Catechism* remains of course just as erroneous as it ever was.

Anyone who will not heed the numerous mutations of Catholic Doctrine contained in the original, and who pays lip service to the necessary alterations made by the Commission of Cardinals, is reading a dangerous book and is culpable of disobedience to the Magisterium in a serious matter.

In this treatise I will accept the fact that the works of Teilhard and the *Dutch Catechism* contain a philosophy in the stricter sense: a system with its own "first principle". I will compare both systems and come to some conclusions. I fully agree with the Editor of *Triumph* magazine:

"Teilhard did not dare to assert his doctrine in the works he attempted to have published during his lifetime. His system can only be understood by studying the privately circulated works. They are the norm." (November 1971)

He is echoing the very words of Pope Pius XII in *Humani Generis*: "In published works some caution is still observed, but more freedom is shown in books privately circulated, in lectures and in meetings for discussion."

Chapter One
Teilhard's System

Dietrich von Hildebrand made the following observation about Teilhard in the famous Appendix to his book *Trojan Horse in the City of God*:

> "I do not know of another thinker who so artfully jumps from one position to another contradictory one, without being disturbed by the jump or even noticing it ..." (p. 275)

He stated a puzzling fact but did not pursue the matter further. However, the question is valid:

If Teilhard did notice these jumps and is apparently not perturbed by them, could this be because he has adopted (invented?) as the foundation of a new philosophy, a new fundamental principle which allows this unperturbed jumping from one position to another contradictory one?

An investigation into this matter, and its startling results, form the subject-matter of this first chapter.

What is Teilhardism? How is it different from any other system? And more specifically: where is the catch? If there is a catch it must be possible to detect it and to express its difference from other systems in simple words that anyone can understand. How could the Catholic Church condemn him as far back as 1922? How could *she* tell the difference? How could she maintain her implacable opposition to his philosophy and "theology" for more than fifty years, while her own children by the millions pored over his books and passed them around?

In three separate papers meant only for private circulation: *Original Sin* (first paper), 1922; *The Human Sense*, 1929; and *Original Sin* (second paper), 1947 Teilhard clearly poses the problem and submits his solution.

(His 1922 essay landed by mistake in Rome where it caused a storm of indignation. After its discovery Teilhard was never again permitted to teach. His highly polished second paper on the same subject (original sin) of 1947, shows that Teilhard never abandoned his system, and personally kept its dissemination and study alive. But the most secret of the three papers, the 1929 paper *The Human Sense*, is the most embarrassing of them all. Until 1971 it had not been published in any language: it contains Teilhard's formal break with the Church.)

In quoting from these three papers I will simply identify them by year. What appears in brackets ( ) was also shown by the publisher of Teilhard's work as such. If I deem emphasis necessary when quoting Teilhard, I will use *italics*. If Teilhard himself uses emphasis, I will show that in **bold**.

Section A

Teilhard's Problem

In the very early stage Teilhard starts by posing the problem like this.

> "I ask myself whether a single man, today, can fit together his view of the geological world evoked by Science, and his view of the world commonly presented by Holy Writ. One cannot keep the two representations, except by passing alternatively from one to the other. Their combination jars; it sounds false. In uniting them on the same plane we are surely victims of an error of perspective." (1922)

We will all readily admit that it is not easy to look at our world with our natural eyes and scientific knowledge, and to look at the same world with the eyes of Supernatural Faith, the way God sees it, as reflected in Holy Writ. However, that is not a new problem. Because of a change of outlook, Teilhard now goes one step further: "**one cannot keep the two representations**". What is this change in outlook? The answer, we will understand more clearly every time we encounter it, lies in what Teilhard means by "**on the same plane**": **evolution**. He clearly expresses here his initial uneasiness of having to maintain **two**. He is well aware that even if we try to unite them in the one world-view (of evolution), we will still have two.

"Since there is no place in the scientific history of the world for the turning-point of Original Sin, since everything happens in our experiential series as if there were neither Adam nor Eden, it follows that the Fall as an event is something unverifiable." (1922)

Here we see Teilhard trace the *modern* problem (of having to maintain a Scientific outlook and a Supernatural view in the same plane: evolution) directly to its origin: Original Sin. And he will stay there, until he has obtained his solution right there. Here at the origin the "two" that caused him so much trouble is the combination of an *apparent absence* of a physical discontinuity in the evolution of the human race with a presence in faith of a supernatural discontinuity of the first magnitude: the Fall. It now starts to become clear that, if for him, "two is a crowd", then which of the two has to go:

"Without exaggeration one can say that Original Sin, in the formulation still current today, is one of the principal obstacles to the intensive and extensive movements of progress in Christian thought. An embarrassment or **scandal** for those of goodwill who are hesitating, and at the same time a refuge for narrow spirits." (1947)

So, the absence of a physical discontinuity (although only apparent) to him became the reason to reject a Supernatural discontinuity: Original Sin. What went on in his mind between 1922 when he rejected the philosophy underlying the Dogma of Original

Sin ("there is no turning-point in human history") and the rejection of the Dogma itself in 1947? His 1929 paper *The Human Sense.*

"The Human Sense believes in a magnificent future of the tangible world, the Gospel seems to disdain it. The Human Sense preaches zest and effort in the conquest of things, Christianity calls for indifference and renunciation. The Human Sense perceives a Universe emerging radiantly from the milieu of struggle for being; Christianity keeps us in the perspective of **a nature fallen and fixed**. Between the Gospel of the theologians and preachers, the Gospel of the Encyclicals or Episcopal letters and the Human Sense there exists at present a deep discord. The Church no longer gives the impression of "thinking with humanity". Such is the profound reason for the atmosphere of hostility that surrounds her. And such is also the explanation of her present sterility ..."

"How will he (i.e. the Christian) continue to find in the same images and the same promises the same satisfaction and the same ardour? He can try to persuade himself that he still believes in the primacy of the Fall, the expiation and the scorn of temporal things: already he is forcing himself **and also he is falsifying himself**. It is a question of perspectives **which we will no longer admit**, because they have become **foreign** to the human soul. No one has ever been able to rekindle a love that has burned out." (1929)

From what I have quoted any Catholic will readily recognize that Teilhard has great difficulty with what trained philosophers will call the *Distinctio Realis* of St Thomas, the "real distinction", one of the fundamental principles of Thomism and incorporated by the Catholic Church in her teachings. To St Thomas and the Catholic Church there exists a real distinction (not only in the human mind, but also *in reality*) between God and Creation, between matter and Spirit, body and soul, between a physical act ("of eating an apple") and the moral act of disobedience to God's Will ("Sin and Fall"), between the natural (the Human Sense, the physical world, science) and the Supernatural (completely unattainable by natural means). Between the Spirit of the Gospel and Holy Writ, and the spirit of the world. The Catholic Church teaches that "contrary truths cannot exist" (Pope John XXIII, *Ad Petri Cathedram*), and so it cannot be true that the Natural and the Supernatural are simultaneously really distinct and really not distinct or the same. It must be either one or the other. But they can form a union since they do not contradict each other, but only over the abyss of the real distinction. And then only if the higher one calls the lower one.

Section B

Teilhard's need for a new philosophical system. His awareness of the consequences

Teilhard is of course well aware that his groping for a solution satisfactory to him must be within a new system with a new fundamental principle. He appears to be equally aware of the consequences: the destruction of Thomism. (See e.g. the final part of the last quote above, 1929, "How will he ...) Also there is the following.

"A collective optimism, realistic and courageous, must definitely replace the pessimism and individualism, whose overgrown notions of **sin** and **personal salvation** have gradually burdened and perverted the Christian spirit ... let us then acknowledge the situation honestly: not only the Imitation of Christ **but also the gospel itself needs to undergo this correction**, and the whole world will make them undergo it. Why not say so?" (1929)

"What increasingly dominates my interest is the effort to establish within myself, and to diffuse around me, a new religion (let's call it an improved Christianity, if you like) whose personal God is no longer the great Neolithic landowner (also translated: proprietor) of times gone by, but the **soul** of the World, as **demanded by the cultural and religious stage we have reached**. (26th January 1936; quoted in *Letters to Zanta*, p 114.)

What is he prepared to pay for all this? As can be expected, nothing of his own, but all that was paid by Infinite Love and the most Precious Blood:

"I have come to the conclusion that, in order to pay for a drastic valorisation and amortisation of the substance of things **a whole series of re-shaping or certain representations or at-**

titudes, which seem to us definitely fixed by Catholic Dogma, has become necessary, if we sincerely wish to Christify Evolution. Seen thus, and because of ineluctable necessity, one could say that a hitherto unknown form of religion is gradually germinating in the heart of Modern Man, in the furrow opened by the idea of Evolution." 1953, (Stuff of the Universe, two years before his death in 1955.)

It was Pope Pius XII who described Teilhard's work as "a cesspool of errors", the same Pope who, three years earlier, had written his encyclical *Humani Generis* against all this.

Section C

The emergence and formulation of the new fundamental principle to underlie Teilhard's synthesis and system

One thing has now become all-important: if Teilhardism in essence means "rejection of the Thomistic, Catholic principle of the real distinction", and if he is well aware that that means a complete new philosophy, theology, religion even, then on what fundamental first principle is he going to build all this, so that Teilhardism becomes, as Cardinal Journet assures us it is, a synthesis, which must be accepted or rejected as a whole.

Let us then start following him in his groping towards this new principle; let us watch him produce it, brush it up and pay for it ...

"Original Sin expresses, translates, personifies in a dated and localized act, the perennial and universal law of failure which is in Humanity by virtue of its being "in fieri" (in evolution). One might go as far as to say, perhaps, that since the creative act (by definition) causes being to mount toward God from the frontiers of Nothingness (that is to say) from the depths of the multiple, **that is from some matter**), all creation entails, as its risk and shadow, some fault, which is to say that it clothes **itself** inevitably with some Redemption. In this conception, the drama of Eden would be the very drama of all human history packed into a symbol profoundly expressive of reality. Adam and Eve are the **symbols** of Humanity on the march towards God. This way of understanding Original Sin obviously eliminates all difficulty of a scientific order (sin becomes bound up with the Evolution of the World)." (1922)

Remember my remarks about brackets ( ) and about **bold**: all the above is Teilhard de Chardin. No wonder this 1922 paper caused a storm in Rome. In passing I draw attention to the fundamental position of Evolution: that God cannot create from nothing, *ex nihilo*, and this according to Teilhard by definition! And now for some comments.

If two things are not **really** distinct, they must be more or less the same. Here we see Teilhard groping towards sameness: he is blurring the edges between the natural (Creation) and the Supernatural (God), between Science and Faith **in the same evolutionary process**. He is obviously looking for some **identity** between all that is really distinct in Thomism, but nevertheless forms a unity. If – as he says – the Fall is nothing more serious than a **mistake** made in a difficult beginning, then it is essentially the **same** as all other mistakes. The idea of sameness (*identitas* in Latin) is already clear in his mind, but he cannot yet announce to the world that they are identical processes, because they obviously are not. The wording of the principle still escapes him, but give him time ...

> "We have just noted that, in the course of the first phase, the official Church tried vainly to bar the path to the natural religion of Effort and Progress. Let us ask if there is not a way of saving both at once (not artificially, but really), of saving the one by the means of the other: the Human Sense and the Christian Spirit. A maladroit course of action has let these two forces come **into opposition**. Should there not be a means of placing them **in natural conjunction** – no longer as hostile forces but as hierarchically arranged energies?" (1929)

> "Isn't it true that for the informed eye these traces have already appeared, insensibly: Original Sin becoming little by little more like a laborious beginning than a Fall: Redemption coming more and more evocative of laborious progress than of expiatory penitence?" (1929)

So there it is, at last, a **sameness in opposition**, a sameness at the same time non-sameness: *Identity in Opposition*. What was in natural opposition must now be made to appear as to be also in **natural conjunction**. This either means a **natural conjunction** with a **sham opposition** ("a *maladroit* course of action", an unfortunate course of action made the Natural and the Supernatural only *appear* to be in opposition); or else **contradiction itself** has now been made into the new principle of evolution.

This impressive sounding principle was worthy of being presented to the world. Teilhard wanted sameness of the natural and the Supernatural without any interference of the hated *distinctio realis*, and this new principle covers the void left by its disappearance. Since no one can live for too long from (or even with) a contradiction, the "in opposition" part would soon be dropped in practise, and only **identity, sameness,** would remain. But the tag "in opposition" sounded impressive enough to ward off the critics.

Contradiction, jumping to contraries, all rolled into one. The most classical way of expressing the **fundamental contradiction** is to state: "non-being is", non-being exists. For this asserts that something simultaneously **is** and **is not**. According to Teilhard, non-being is a pure state, and also, since we may replace "Multiple" by "non-being", we may also read: **non-being** is the sole rational form ... making use of the fundamental contradiction to make a statement. Something that does not exist: a non-being (even in a pure state!) at the same time is something: "is a form ...". If his new principle allows this sort of thing: an identity in opposition to being and non-being, then his first principle itself must be a contradiction.

He again denies God the power to create from nothing, as again he clearly states that "to create" means a rearrangement and unification of a pre-existing primordial mass of non-being.

He also makes the jump from "to create is to unify" to its contrary "union creates" as if these two statements are the same, as if he is saying "If you don't object to the second statement, how could you object to the first?" But let us listen a bit more.

> "In such a universe in which the Multiple is the primordial non-sinful creatable form of Nothingness: **the functional equivalent of the first Adam, source of statistical evil**, the (intellectual) problem of evil disappears. Since in this perspective, in effect, physical suffering and moral faults are introduced **inevitably** (his stress) into the world, not because of some defect of the creative act, but because of the very structure of participated being (that is, under the heading of a **by-product, statistically inevitable** (his stress) of the unification of the multiple ...etc. etc" (1947)

> "In this explanation Original Sin undoubtedly ceases to be an isolated act ..." (1947)

It also ceases to be a sin.

Not much is left over of the First Adam: he is nothing but nothingness, the Multiple, a primordial mass, a source of statistical evil. It does not make the Second Adam look very impressive either.

And so we stumble upon yet another name of this "mystical" principle: "**unity in opposition**". If the creative act of Almighty God ceases to be really distinct from any other (human) act of unification, since God's act presupposes exactly the same as any other act of unification: **something pre-existing to be unified**, then we in evolution, helping God along with science, in the unification of the universe, **are thus creating**. This is the foundation of Teilhard's pantheism.

We are now in a better position to appreciate the *vital concern* expressed by so many popes, about a **dilution** of Thomism, to say nothing of its **abolition**: the result is sheer nonsense.

Section D

The implications of this discovery

Before we deal in the next chapter with the vital question: Did any of this ever get a foothold in any of the Philosophy courses, or even in the Theology courses, anywhere in the world? (to which, regrettably, the answer is Yes), I would like, in this Section D, to pause for a moment, and let the enormity of what we have discovered sink in.

I. The World-Wide Spread

It seems obvious that throughout the world millions of Catholics and protestants have been caught up in this system and have been affected by its poison, yet they never got it from reading Teilhard. In fact many would not even notice that their whole thinking has been put in a different direction or alignment.

Teilhard taught *the world at large* how to live from a contradiction, and the world in turn taught its children. How to direct one's thinking from a contradiction: how to call at last the Supernatural, natural; how to call a sin "a statistical mistake" or an "inevitable by-product of creation"; how to call impurity a "new form of love"; how to see the difference between protestants and Catholics as a "unity in opposition" with very little opposition and a lot of fundamental "sameness": the basis of the false ecumenism. Or: how to call "following your own conscience" a new and higher form of obedience to the Church or to one's Superiors. And finally: how to call love for the world the **new** and **higher** form of love for God ...

No wonder his message spread like wildfire through the length and breadth of a mesmerized world, which deliriously drank in his "gospel of liberation from the yoke of the old Christianity-gone-wrong", thinking they were doing a favour and service to God ... Who still cares about the rest of his absurd system: the "creabile", the "multiple", the "noosphere"? What matters is, that contradictions no longer count, that sin is no longer sin, and that the more we plough into this world and embrace it in evolution to help it along a bit, the more we apparently please God and discover Him. If this evolution is the new Christianity, then surely this evolution must be good.

And so each one can now build his own popular philosophy on his own popular contradiction (conscience, the pill, free love, making money ...) on the authority of this new prophet, call it the "new" philosophy, the "new" theology, the "new" Christianity: and lo and behold: you are part of this "new" faith in the World and Evolution ... "until the dawn of nothingness".

To make matters infinitely worse for Catholics: Walter M. Abbot S.J. in his *The Documents of Vatican II*, pp. 269-270, footnote, declares categorically that we have no hope of understanding "this document of Vatican II" (*The Church in The Modern World* –

Gaudium et spes) unless we read Teilhard's *Le Milieu Divin*, and understand his *nouvelle theologie*. So, what the Holy Spirit gave us in Vatican II must be seen and understood through the writings of a man with more than fourteen censures and condemnations (including one Encyclical) against his works from the same Holy Spirit. If that is not "directing one's thinking from a contradiction" then I do not know what is. *Le Milieu Divin* has been steadfastly refused an imprimatur from the Holy See ever since it was conceived in 1926; not withstanding relentless pressure from all sides. And that was not the first time Fr. Abbot tried to interest his readers in Teilhard: another footnote with his name in it appeared earlier, on p. 204.

What proved impossible during the Sessions of Vatican II: that the Council would be wrenched away from the direct protection of the Holy Spirit against heresy, was to a large extent accomplished afterwards, when the thousands of sympathizers and admirers of Teilhard got hold of the interpretations of Vatican II (IDOC!) and made us look at Vatican II from Teilhard's fundamental contradiction. Fr. Abbot is a classic case in point.

Since no one can live too long from (or even with) a contradiction as already stated, all the popular "identities in opposition" or "unity in opposition philosophies", sprung up after the Council under the direct inspiration of Teilhard, soon drop their "in opposition" part with two grave consequences.

1. The unity, identity, without opposition, and no longer protected by the real distinction, are in grave danger of giving to the world its false ecumenism as a direct result from

Teilhardism, **but assumed to come from Vatican II** because of the switch in interpretation; and

2. If the Teilhard doctrine: "Love for the world (the world seen in evolution), no longer really distinct from God, with God incarcerated in it as its soul) is identical in opposition to love of God", becomes (after dropping the "in opposition" bit): "Love of the World is identical to love of God" (which is quite acceptable nowadays), then all who follow Teilhard in adhering to this contradiction, are now in direct opposition to the Catholic Church of two thousand years, which has always taught us that God so loved the world that He sent His only Son to die for the Redemption of the world. The modernists like the first bit, but reject the last part (which then completely changes the meaning of the first part) and they are not prepared to follow Christ and His Church in their self-sacrifice for the sake of souls. And so anyone who looks at the Catholic Church through the eyes and works of Teilhard, openly recommended even in footnotes, will only see his own church take shape: the church of evolution, the church of no sin, no dogma, the church of contradiction: the church of anti-Christ.

II. What is at the Bottom of all this?

"I shall put enmity between thee and the Woman and between thy seed and Hers."

With these Words God, "before whom a thousand years are but one day", indicated that the fundamental contradiction between

Good and Evil would remain Absolute, so that neither evil could ever be good, nor good ever be evil; no matter what future generations would call it, or would make it appear to be. He also pointed out that there is a high (although only created) intelligence behind evil and that it is to be expected, that over the history of the world, this intelligence behind evil would finally be capable of mounting a highly organized drive.

Organized global evil cannot tolerate next to itself, and not under its control, the existence of two things: a Supernatural Catholic Faith, and an Infallible Pope. According to Vatican I, the first one is the *Radix* (root) and *Fundamentum* (foundation) of Supernatural Life and Sanctification, the latter is the root and foundation of Absolute Truth. The more Catholics will be imbued with the spirit of evolution, the more they will be weaned away from these two fundamental bulwarks against a global victory of evil.

How does Teilhard and his system fit into this?

The thwarting of these plans for world domination is obviously a Grace of truly global dimensions. Like all graces, this one too *is not forced* upon us, but is to be prayed for and prepared for. For Catholics, the external temptation, as a test for their sincerity towards the preparation and reception of this singular grace, was Teilhard and his "system". God would make it clear right at the start of these absurd ideas and theories (1922) and at every major stage of their development (more than fourteen times) **that these theories could not be listened to, accepted and spread about,** *unless in Disobedience to the lawful teaching authority* within the Catholic Church. But like with all great temptations (with their corresponding repercussions either way): these theories and ideas constituted a **real delight** for the proud Modern Mind ...

The penalty for yielding became, inevitably, in the natural order an abject mental blindness of no longer recognizing as **degrading** the acceptance of a **contradiction** for the direction of one's life. And in the Supernatural order it became a spiritual blindness resulting from the loss of one's Catholic Faith. On both scores, they, to whom the continuation of the work of Salvation was entrusted, became themselves easy prey for the global enslavers.

Make no mistake: God is not mocked. After the Original Sin of our first parents, God revealed the most fundamental real distinction of them all: the contradiction between good and evil. It immediately follows that all who follow Teilhard in his second Original Sin: teaching the rejection of a real Adam, a real Eve, a real Sin committed by them, in order to accept his unscientific evolution: that all those are not only punished by God, they are passing **on the fruits** of their original sin to our children in the form of spurious catechetics.

The rule is very simple: anyone who no longer lives by, nor fully accepts the teachings of Pope Pius XII, right down the line, say, to the Council of Trent, including all that the popes taught us on Thomism: such a person sees Vatican II through the eyes of Teilhard and was almost certainly taught to do that. Invariably you will find such a person believe in a contradiction. He may not even be aware of it. They usually explain and exaggerate the **unity** of things to such an extent, that there is no longer any room for a real distinction (mainly in the area of "Catholic Faith" and "Christian Faith") which then leads to contradictions.

On the other hand: if you can find a person who still prayerfully accepts all the Catholic Church's teachings, including Vatican II, and including her condemnations of Teilhard de Chardin, you will find that such a person will look at Vatican II with the eyes of Catholic Faith, and he will see and explain Vatican II in the light of all the previous teachings, as requested by the Holy Spirit.

Chapter Two

The Spread of Teilhard's System
over Catholic Institutes of Higher Learning

It is of the utmost importance to study the spread of Teilhard's ideas from the very beginning. The acceptance of his ideas, theories and principles is as world-wide as the global conquest of evil. The conclusion has become inescapable that it is now part of that evil. Teilhardism proved to be the only weapon in the arsenal of the plotters capable of penetrating to any great extent the Catholic Church through the least likely of bastions: the seminaries.

However, the study of this Chapter Two is not necessary for the reading and understanding of the final chapter: the influence of Teilhard on the *Dutch Catechism*. I inserted the contents of this chapter here for the sake of continuity and chronology. If the reader finds the going a bit tough, he or she can let the matter rest for a while without endangering the understanding of the next and final chapter. He or she can come back to the present chapter later and take his or her time with it.

It is the task of this second chapter to see in detail how the principles of Teilhard have penetrated the philosophy courses of the Jesuit College *Berchmanianum*, in Nijmegen, Holland. No doubt the capture of Louvain came first, as Teilhard had there two of his very few trusted friends within the Society of Jesus: Père Charles and Père Marechal. But the rapport between Nijmegen and Louvain had always been cordial.

I will be quoting from the official notes and theses as handed down between the years 1943 and 1947 by the Jesuit Professors of *Logica Major* (the study of Truth and its principles); of *Psychologia Rationalis* (theoretical psychology or anthropology: the study of man); and of *Ethica* (or Ethics: the study of the principles underlying the actions of man in his striving after his final destiny; the principles of the moral order).

(To see this in context: it was in 1946 already that the Jesuits of Louvain, after having studied and debated for years the privately circulated documents of Teilhard, set up the *Lumen Vitae* course in modern catechetics entirely on his principles. It was Fr. Charles who, according to Teilhard himself in his letters, did everything possible to have *Le Milieu Divin* published with Ecclesiastical approval. Since 1948 Louvain was quite openly teaching *polygenism* or *polygenesis* (the theory that the human race originated in several places at once over the globe), thereby showing ready acceptance of Teilhard's synthesis.)

Within this chapter I hope to highlight three important aspects:

1. If the philosophy taught there in Nijmegen and Louvain during all those years had become contaminated, then it could only support later on an erroneous theology with grave danger to Catholic Faith, as warned by the encyclicals and letters of many popes.

2. And if it was this new, erroneous theology which gave birth to the *Dutch Catechism* (DC) with its world-wide repercussions, then the DC too will contain the basic flaws and contradictions of Teilhard's system.

3. This, finally, shows up the fallacy in the following line of defence sometimes adopted: "This whole Teilhard business is of no concern to anyone who never read his books." Unfortunately, this is not so. Teilhard's aberrations have been spread about so insidiously and so thoroughly in all sorts of publications – in defiance of the Church's clear directives – that his system is almost breathed in, soaked up, wherever we go. We need a continuous conscious effort not to acquiesce to some contradiction.

Section A

Teilhard de Chardin's influence on the
Philosophy of Truth (Logic) Course
(a first year subject)

The course in Logic, *Metaphysica Veritatis*, or the Philosophy of Truth was divided into two main parts: Does Truth exist? (*An sit veritas*) and "What is Truth" (*Quid sit veritas*). Since the two questions are intimately related one has to start with a working definition, which, according to St Thomas is: "*Veritas est adaequatio rei et intellectus*", or: Truth is an adaptation of a thing and an intellect, a matching. Two things are brought out here: (a) St Thomas knows there is a real distinction between an object known, and the mind knowing it. (b) St Thomas also knows the word "*identitas*", sameness in every respect, and does not hesitate to use that word, if necessary. Here he uses another word: "*adequatio*", matching, adaptation, some sort of equality. If, according to St Thomas my knowledge of an object matches the object itself, then I call that relation Truth, and the knowledge truthful.

At the end of this first part of the course, consisting of three theses concerning the existence of Truth, the following pages are entirely devoted to the study of the First Principle, a "theory" so new, that, although it ought to have been a complete thesis, with its formal proofs, it was not quite ready yet to be presented as a thesis. However, it was treated and presented as anything but a theory.

For the benefit of interested experts who may read these pages, I will quote the original text *verbatim* in the Latin in which it was presented to the students followed by my English translation.

(*Thesis*) **4a**

Primum pricipium metaphysicum est principium **identitas** *quo identitas idealitatis cum realitate exprimutur; iustifcatur ex hoc quod est expressio ipsius naturae intellectus; eo ipso etiam patet cur sit principium immediate evidens.*

4th thesis

The first principle in Philosophy is the principle of **identity** by which the identity between ideas (in the mind) and reality is expressed; its justification lies in the fact that it expresses the very nature of the (human) intellect itself; it is for that same reason clear why it is an immediately evident (self-evident) principle.

No. **1.** *Vidimus affirmationem veritatis quae est expressio realititas, esse necessarium. Vivit enim illa affirmatio in omni actu cognitionis, quatenus in omni affirmatione, negatione, dubitatione, cet., affirmatur absoluta relatio intellectus ad ordinem objectivam realem.*

No. **1.** We saw that affirming the existence of truth, which gives expression to reality, cannot be withheld. For the simple reason that this affirmation is found in every act of knowing as in every affirmation, denial, doubt, etc., the absolute relation between the intellect and the real, objective order is acknowledged.

No. **2.** *Questioni "an sit verititas" affirmative respondemus. Haec necessaria relatio exprimitur per principium quod vocatur* **principium identititas**: *esse est cognoscible, veritas est, verum est ens, ens est verum, vel uti generaliter ponitur: esse est, ens est ens, quod est, est.*

No. **2.** To the question: "does truth exist" we replied in the affirmative. This necessary relation is mirrored by the principle which carries the name the **principle of identity**: being is knowable, truth exists, what is true must exist, what is must be true, or as expressed more generally: to be, is; a being (reality) is a being (in the mind, known), or simply that what exists, is.

No. **3.** *Illud principium est non tantum lex fundamentalis idealitatis (logicae) sed etiam realititas (ontologicae) quae in hoc principio communi its unituntur, ut omnis scepticismus radicitus refutetur.*

No. **3.** This principle is not only the fundamental law of what exists in the mind (of logics) but also of the real (of ontologics) which through this principle they have in common, that all scepticism is radically refuted.

The remaining seven (7) sub-sections of this fourth thesis are devoted to the development of these ideas. Explanations are sustained with numerous quotes from contemporary authors: Fr. Marechal (Louvain, intimate of Teilhard, and quoted from his strange "cahier": *Le Pointe de Depart de la Metaphysique*), Blondel,

Fr. K Rahner, S.J., Fr. Geny, S.J., Prof Dondeyne (Louvain) etc. The most striking aspect of this whole "thesis" is, that occasionally St Thomas is mentioned and never quoted in his own words, but through the words of all these modern authors **as they understood his words**. Only reference numbers of places are quoted from St Thomas, where if you are interested, you can look up what St Thomas has to say. That this is not only misleading, but definitely open for misrepresentation and even fraud, we will soon see an example of.

The reason why St Thomas is not quoted in his own words is obvious: he cannot be quoted to sustain what is being developed here. St Thomas speaks about an *adaequatio*, which is a synthesis over an underlying real distinction. He never speaks of an ontological identity on the human level, nor between the natural and supernatural. His ideas are totally unacceptable to the framers of this *thesis quarta*, which does not teach Thomism as requested by the popes. A quick run through will show this.

No. **2.** Explanation of the notion of the first principle. No quotes from St Thomas.

No. **3.** This is the most important sub-section: it deals with the ontological identity (a complete sameness in being) between the principle of knowing and the principle of being. It starts with the remark that many authors admit various first principles as no one principle can adequately express the enormous complexity of existence, being. But then the author states immediately that underneath the variety of principles, there is nevertheless only **one** first principle: this principle of **identity**, otherwise the underlying unity cannot be explained. By now he is forced to call it an absolute identity between what is in the mind (*idealitas*) and what is outside the mind (*realitas*):

Theses precedents iam in lucem posuerunt absolutam relationem inter cognosecere et esse, inter idealitatem et realititatem.

"The previous theses have already brought to light that there exists an absolute relation between knowing and being, between what is in the mind and in reality."

A quote in German from Fr. Rahner's book *Spirit in the World* then follows to substantiate this doctrine. We have now reached the climax: it is so important that I will quote *verbatim* what is printed.

*Ad hoc autem requiritur ut adsit quaedam originaria unio inter esse et cognoscere its ut, ubi sit esse, ibi sit cognito et vice versa. Haec unio non potest esse **quaedam** relatio quae tum esse tum cognoscere subsequeretur, quia tunc factum unitatis inter esse cognoscere **in omni actu cognitionis** intelligi non posset.*

Haec etiam est doctrina constans St Thomae.

"For this, however, it is required that there exists some original union between "being" and "knowing" so that, where there is being, there is knowing and vice versa. This union cannot be **any** relation to which both being and knowing would comply, as then the fact of the unity between to be and to know **in every act of knowing** could not be understood.

This is also the consistent doctrine of St Thomas."

And now, at last, we might get some quotations from the Angelic Doctor himself, as he is called by the Church. But no, we get immediately a quotation in German from the same book of Fr. Rahner, telling us what Fr. Rahner thinks is the meaning of St Thomas. I will quote him in English:

"Being and knowing are in an original unity. Knowing is not an approximate 'hitting on' its object. St Thomas expressedly rejects the vulgar notion of knowing as 'just coming across' something. Knowing does not happen '*per contactum intellectus ad rem intelligibilem*' (by contact of the intellect with an object that can be known), on the contrary: according to St Thomas 'to be (or being) and to know (or knowing) are the same': '***idem intellectus et intellectum et intelligere***' (the intellect, and the understood, and understanding itself are identical).

Strong language. The mind of the Professor and the mind of Fr. Rahner could not be expressed more clearly. **But the world-famous place in St Thomas, where St Thomas teaches that the mind, the object in the mind and the act of understanding are all the same, identical, is not indicated.** The Professor, in his notes, then goes on:

"In amongst many places of St Thomas, you can, if you wish, look up Summa Theologica I, q. 14, art. 2, c.; q. 27, a, 1, ad 2; q. 34, a. 1, ad. 3; q. 55, a. 1 ad 2; q. 85, a. 2 ad 1; q. 87, a. 1, ad 3."

After these it was then stated, rather nonchalantly:

"There are also several texts in *De Veritate* (another work by St Thomas), *Summa Contra Gentiles* (another work again), etc."

That's all. No specifications where, in these works, these supremely important statements can be found. So I looked up the texts in St Thomas as quoted above, and I found Fr. Rahner's famous text of St Thomas: "*idem intellectus et intellectum*" (the mind and what is in the mind are identical) in *Summa Theologica* I, question 34, article 1, ad 3 (as quoted above), where St Thomas says:

In Deo autem importat omnimodam identitam, quia in Deo est omnio idem intellectus et intellectum, ut supra ostensum est (q. 14, art. 2 and 4).

which translated gives the true mind of St Thomas:

"**In God**, however, (knowing, understanding) brings out an identity in every respect (*omnimoda*), because **in God** the intellect and what is in the intellect (what is known) are completely identical, as we have shown earlier in q. 14, art. 2 and 4."

And that makes all the difference: **only in God**, according to St Thomas, **can we speak of an identity between** *idealitas* **and** *realitas*. Exactly the same doctrine of St Thomas is set forth in the other places mentioned. No wonder the Professor and Fr. Rahner did not quote the words of St Thomas: these two wanted us to believe, by misquoting St Thomas, that the Angelic Doctor teaches that **al-**

ways, everywhere, the intellect and what is in the intellect are identical. With Teilhard, they want **identity** to be the foundation of **every union,** and also they want to show themselves to be Thomistic. But St Thomas **will never admit to an** *identitas* between Creation and God nor between the acts of creatures and their faculties. This fourth thesis is no longer the teaching of St Thomas, but of Teilhard. To make this quite clear, this sub-section 3 of this fourth thesis concludes precisely on this note:

> *Si autem inter idealitatem et realitatem, inter cognitionem et esse, adest identitas, omne ens est ideale quid, et omne ideale est aliquid reale.*
>
> "If however between *idealitas* and *realitas* (what is in the mind and what is outside the mind) there exists an identity, as in between the "the known" and "the existing", all existing is somehow ideal, and all that is in the mind, exists.

Next in sub-sections **4** and **5** the serious charges of contradiction and *panpsychism* are touched upon and simply denied.

Sub-section **6** deals with the obvious problem that, although we are an identity *idealitas* and *realitas* (but not according to St Thomas, as we saw) we do not know everything. As can be expected from the followers of Teilhard, this brings out the **opposition** aspect in the identity, based on an imperfect intuition. But the Professor hastens to undo the meaning of this opposition, in case the true meaning of real distinction had to come out: by stressing the underlying unity, exactly as Teilhard did. Otherwise, if the opposition was **real**, the underlying unity could not be understood.

Ut autem intellectus illam synthesim exprimere posit, requir-
itur ut ipse intellectus **natura sua sit synthesis** *idealitatis et re-*
alitatis.

"In order that the intellect can express the synthesis, it is
required that, by its very nature, the intellect itself **IS** the synthesis between idealitas and realitas."

And in No. **7.**

Ita lumen **quod nosmetipsi sumus,** *fundamentum est omnis*
cognitionis nostrae, non autem **adhuc** *ultimum fundamentum.*
Detegimus (his stress) enim nosmetipsos ut identitatem inter
idealitatem et realitatem, hoc est not intuitive sed iudicative (in
weak opposition that does not affect the fundamental identity).

"And so the light **that we are ourselves,** is the foundation
of all our knowledge but *not yet* our final foundation. We *dis-*
cover ourselves as an identity not by intuition but by judgement
..."

The proud modern mind: we are our own identity. We are our
own light. Is this only an unfortunate choice of words to explain in
modern ways the fundamental doctrine of St Thomas? Inadmissi-
ble, as the fundamental doctrine of St Thomas is no longer coming
out, but is rather made to look incongruous because of the complete switch in fundamental positioning: what St Thomas only ap-
plies to God, we saw the modern Fr. Rahner apply indiscriminately
to all knowledge. The result is obvious: to obviate the fundamental
contradiction awaiting anyone who turns his back on Thomism:

The non-God (creature) = God. In the absence of the *distinctio realis*, the fundamental unity must be stressed, by which it is denied that the creature is non-God. So then we end up with an equation like this: creature = God, which is Teilhard's pantheism. And just as much a contradiction. On this philosophy there is no real Supernatural (*Le Milieu Divin* is then the *milieu* among the God-creatures), no Fall, no Sin, no need for the Cross, Expiation Redemption, or even personal salvation (that "perversion", we heard Teilhard call it), no Dogma (we are our own light), no Catholic Church. The philosophy of this fourth thesis is Teilhard de Chardin, and it became the philosophy in preparation for the *Dutch Catechism*.

Section B

Teilhard de Chardin's influence on the
Theoretical Psychology Course
(*a second year subject*)

After our rather extensive treatment of Teilhard's influence on the Philosophy of Truth, we can now be satisfied that nothing fundamentally different will be taught in the other disciplines which make up the complete philosophy course of Nijmegen and Louvain: the philosophy of fundamental **identity**. So in treatment of the next two examples, I would like to draw attention to aspects, peculiar to each, which shed abundant additional light on Teilhard's influence.

In his already mentioned Appendix, Dietrich von Hildebrand (a Professor of Philosophy himself for many years), draws attention to a characteristic of Teilhard's system where it differs sharply from Thomism:

> "Teilhard sees 'self-consciousness' as the only difference between man and a highly developed animal. But the comparison of the limited type of consciousness that can be observed in animals with the manifold aspects of a **person's** consciousness shows instantly how wrong it to regard the latter as merely an addition of *self*-consciousness ... But the marvel of the human mind ... is altogether lost on Teilhard because he insists on viewing human consciousness as merely an *awareness* of self that has gradually developed out of animal consciousness. The Scholastics, on the other hand, accurately grasped the dimensions of personal consciousness by calling a person a being that *possesses* itself."

From this misconception of human person, Teilhard draws the only logical – but nevertheless equally erroneous – conclusion: that a collective consciousness would constitute a **higher state** of evolution as "explained" clearly in *The Phenomenon of Man*, where the acceptance of a **non-individual consciousness** is one more example of his fundamental contradiction.

Why I quote all this becomes immediately clear, if one reads the very first thesis in this second course, which purports to deal with the most fundamental concept of Man (again: whose fundamental concept?).

Thesis 1a

Homo, qui in vita sese experitur tamquam totalitatem sui con-sciam, ope reflectionis sese detegit tamquam aliquid substantiale.

1ˢᵗ thesis

Man, who in this life, experiences himself as a totality **aware of himself**, with the aid of reflection discovers himself to be self-sufficient.

1. *Agitur in hac thesi de astruendo fundamento totius psychlogiae.*

"With this thesis it is meant to lay the foundation of the whole psychology course."

These last words make it clear that the Professor wants to base the whole psychology course, which is a fundamental course on Man, on *self-awareness*. This man is at least honest enough to admit that, in doing this, he is not following St Thomas, when he confesses at the end of his formal proof:

5. *Quoad textus S. Thomae dicendum est argumentum in frma quam deminus* **non inveniri.**

"As for the texts of St Thomas, it must be stated that, in the form in which we put it, they **cannot be found**."

So Professor von Hildebrand was right: Thomism does not put the human person, in his distinction from animals, merely on a basis of *self-awareness*. It is by now equally obvious that the con-struer of this thesis was familiar with the more fundamental prin-ciples of Teilhard's system, where these ideas are to be found. I will now very briefly touch on this second thesis, where the fundamen-tal doctrine of *identitas* is faithfully adhered to.

In this second thesis it will be admitted that:

... in homine adest quaedam duplicitas quae tamen unitatem non subvertit.

" ... in man there exists some duality, which does not upset the unity."

The explanation of this starts off by pointing out that "the human substance (*substantia humana*) has revealed itself to us in the first thesis as an identity between subject and object, or between *idealitas* and *realitas*". However, in man this **identity** is in **opposition**. The basis of this opposition is again blamed on the imperfect way in which *intuition* is realized in man. And then follows the classic way in which the *distinctio realis* is done away with:

Unde in substantia cocreta partes hae tum realiter a se distinguuntur tum etiam realiter idem sunt.

"And so, in the concrete existence of the human subsistence, the composing parts are not only really distinct: they are also **really the same**."

A splendid contradiction, as expected. All the talk about *distinctio realis* is nullified by the deliberate teaching of the "mutual priority" principle between the composing parts that make out Man.

Finally, St Thomas gets the same short shrift as in the Logic course: merely a mention where something, that is being taught here, can be found. And so it goes on ...

Section C

Teilhard de Chardin's influence on the
Ethics Course
(a third year subject)

This course too had its own particular modernistic aspect, apart from the general debility, so manifest in the other two courses already discussed. To put it in perspective, I will quote from Pope Pius XII's Encyclical *Humani Generis*, (on Modern Errors) of 12th August 1950, remembering that this Ethics course was studied in 1946. (I do not know if it was subsequently re-written in light of this Encyclical).

> "No wonder if this spirit of innovation has already borne poisonous fruits in almost every sphere of theology. ... Others destroy the gratuitous character of the supernatural order, by suggesting that it would be impossible for God to create rational beings without equipping them for the beatific vision and calling them to it."

But this is precisely the doctrine of this Ethics course. It is a bit beyond the scope of this treatise to go into detail of *how* the *desiderium naturale* versus *supernaturalitatem* was proved to be connatural to man, from which it follows that human nature could not be conceived to exist without it. Although the thesis on this – the third thesis – expressedly declared "that the beatific vision exceeds the natural powers and demands of man", according to the pope "the gratuitous character of the supernatural order" is already destroyed by the first part of the thesis which taught that it is essential to human nature to strive for the beatific vision.

With the first three theses the evolutionary trend of the course was established, showing Teilhard's influence in the blurring of the edges between the natural and the supernatural, as right from the start the real distinction between the natural ultimate goal of man and his supernatural goal was denied. Since the author of the theses boldly declares that St Thomas is on his side, and since, again, he too refuses to print the very words of St Thomas, and only indicates where they can be found, I will print the beginning of the third thesis in full, and only in Latin.

(*Thesis*) 3a

Beatitudo simpliciter perfects hominis specificativa sumpta consistit in cognitione **intuitiva** *(my stress) Divinae Essentiae: haec tamen beatitudo superat ones vires et exigenitas naturales hominis et omnis naturae creatae.*

Acriter scholastici de has parte thesos inter se disputant.

Nobis consentiunt: (a) S. Thomas: I, 12, 1; I-II, 3, 8; III c.G, 50 ...

Nobis adversantur: (b) R. Garrigou-Lagrange ...

If one looks up the two places referred to here in St Thomas, all we read is that St Thomas teaches that man has a natural desire to know God *naturally*, that is, on his (man's) natural level. He wants to come to a knowledge of God here on earth because of the inquisitive nature of his intellect. (This is nothing but the doctrine of St Paul in his Letter to the Romans). Nowhere does St Thomas say that man wants an **intuitive vision of God** in the supernatural order. All St Thomas says about that is: if someone denies that the saints in heaven can see God, then that is not true.

And so it is clear that Pope Pius XII, in refuting the claim made by this modernistic author, is certainly not contradicting St Thomas. The real distinction between the natural order and the fully gratuitous supernatural order (which begins with the supernatural act of Divine Catholic Faith), is complete, absolute and wholly maintained by St Thomas.

So there was a second example of deliberate misquotation of St Thomas to 'prove' him on the side of Teilhard de Chardin errors.

This concludes the second chapter of this essay. It shows from internal evidence and criticism that the philosophy course studied in those days was definitely modernistic, incorporated the fallacies and pitfalls of Teilhard, was guilty of misquotations of the authentic teachings of St Thomas, and contained patent elements in need of rebuke and correction by a pope. It proved to be a most unsuitable foundation for the subsequent theology that gave to the world the *Dutch Catechism.*

Chapter Three

The Influence of Teilhard de Chardin
on the Dutch Catechism

If the *Dutch Catechism* (DC) is built on a Teilhard de Chardin philosophy and 'theology', then according to Cardinal Journet, it will form the same synthesis or system; it will be built on the same contradiction and will prove to be just as uncompromising as Teilhardism itself. The difficulty the good cardinals experienced trying to "fit some Thomistic theology into it" is a pointer in that direction. Maybe they could have saved themselves the trouble: it certainly appears as if the catechism must be rejected or accepted as it stands. But strong pointers as all these things are, they only amount to circumstantial evidence, as does the long list of its shortcomings. The DC stands accused by all of this: gravely accused. But in order to be rejected *in toto* it must stand condemned. It must be proven guilty. If the DC is Teilhardism in catechetical garb, then it must yield its secret and reveal the same contradiction as was discovered to lie at the root of the "master-vision" - and found at the bottom of everything inspired by it. In order to make it do this, we will turn our attention first to the DC's most vulnerable part: its Philosophy of Man.

Section A

The Dutch Catechism's Concept of Man

"The life in my body comes from the beasts" (p. 10)

The author (Fr. P. Schoonenberg, S.J.) bases himself here on Evolution. We also see him use words which we know have a special meaning in the philosophy, theology and dogma of the Catholic Church. We may call this system "Hallowed Thomism". (Thomism as a philosophy only, remains a philosophical system; but if the Catholic Church takes up the meaning of a term, or a doctrine in Thomism for the formulation of her dogmas, then we can truly speak of "hallowed Thomism"). In chapters one and two of this essay I compared the philosophical system called "Thomism" with a philosophical system called "Teilhardism". In the discussion here on the DC we must accept Thomism in its wider sense, and compare the doctrine of the DC with what I call here "hallowed Thomism".

Now one thing is clear: evolutionism and Thomism are absolutely incompatible. They are both systems, using their own principles and language (jargon). One destroys the other because they are contradictory systems. Now right throughout this book, the DC, the authors try to **explain an evolutionist religion using Thomistic terms**, hallowed by their use in the Catholic Church. Terms such as life, body, God, creation, man, Christ, resurrection, spirit, soul, ... They use these Thomistic terms trying to give meaning to a contrary system. But "contradictory truths cannot exist" (Pope John XXIII): evolution and Thomism **cannot both be true.**

And so the result, as was to be expected, is an abysmal failure to explain either system. The lip service paid to the doctrine of the Catholic Faith fails dismally to save the essence of the Catholic Faith (as if it was in need of "being saved"), and fails equally to make the contrary doctrine of evolution come to life. Modernists never allow us to show how their theories contradict Dogma and Revelation, because to them neither dogma nor Revelation **ought to be expressed in Thomistic terms**, no matter what the popes have said about that. Meanwhile they make full use of the liberty of expressing their ideas in Thomistic terms, which by the use in the Church have received definite, all-time meanings **pertaining to the salvation of souls.**

Since they select to fight this battle on Thomistic use of words but with evolutionistic meanings, we accept the challenge and show their contradictions using the same words with their normal and hallowed meaning.

But make no mistake: there is hardly a single word in the whole English language which has the same meaning in Evolutionism as in Thomism. They intend to write a catechism of the future, where the whole of dogma (so they claim) will be retranslated in the words and meanings of evolutionary theory, as postulated by Teilhard himself, as we saw, when he said:

> "I have come to the conclusion that, in order to pay for a drastic valorization and amortization of the substance of things, a whole series of re-shaping of certain representations or attitudes, which seem to us definitely fixed by Catholic dog-

ma, has become necessary, if we sincerely wish to Christify Evolution."

The present DC is a first attempt to break the barriers "and to get us used to it". They fervently hope that, once Thomism is destroyed with its real distinction principle, the formidable, ugly contradiction on which evolution is built, will cease to exist and will disappear forever. They forget that Dogma is *Verbum Dei*, and no longer Thomism ...

And now back to the first quotation, above. It is a case in point: evolutionists mean by "life" and "body" something completely different from ordinary Christian use. So the authors will try to explain and explain, going round and round in circles, endlessly, writing a 500 page book with very little substance in it. (Sorry about that Thomistic word.)

I'll start once more:

"The life in my body comes from the beasts" (p. 10)

This means two things: (a) 'life' and 'body' are not the same, so a distinction is made here by the authors; and (b) at least one of them: 'life', comes from the beasts (Remember that, even if teilhardists make a distinction, they totally reject a real distinction. *Will it be the same here?*)

"And richer and richer finds showed still more clearly the great drama of the spine slowly straightened up, and the skull that took a greater volume as the beast developed into man." (p. 10)

We are told here quite clearly by the use of words such as "spine" and "skull", that the body of man also came from the beasts. Since "soul" is not to be admitted quite explicitly in this catechism, as we will see, they tell us here that the *whole* man comes from the beasts. (Remember also that **we are not allowed to show that they contradict Catholic Dogma**: that is meaningless to them.) So we will do something far more deadly to them.) To reinforce their evolutionary doctrine, we are told on p. 470:

"Death is the end of the whole man as we know him."

We know him as having life and body: all that comes from the beasts, so according to this catechism, quite logically: he ends up as the beasts end up. All this must of course be "squared off" with "Thomism and Dogma", hence the pages and pages of writing to explain away their contradiction that there is such a thing as "Resurrection". Resurrection is *no* difficulty in Thomism and the Catholic Church: it becomes a grave contradiction in evolutionism. Before I go on to a discussion on "soul", I would like to select a few more quotations on "life":

"On the contrary: it gives us life ..." (p. 500)

No where does the author talk about "divine life": there is no room for it since we have no soul, so life is identical with Life.

There is no real distinction between the natural and the Supernatural. But that "it" in this quote which is supposed to be giving life, is not referring to the beasts: so beasts and non-beasts are giving us life.

"... as they give new life to the child." (p. 382)

The "they" here are the parents. So, apparently, my parents are beasts, since p. 10 told me: "the life in *my body* comes from the beasts." And if my parents are not beasts, then the life in my body comes from beasts and non-beasts at the same time: a classical contradiction. **Anything at all except the Truth: God created me.**

As can be seen from what we have uncovered so far: just as Cardinal Journet assured us, one cannot pick and choose from Teilhardism; neither can that be done from Catholic Dogma, nor from Thomism. One fundamental contradiction is enough to evoke a whole army of contradictions. E.g. how do they see the Conception of Our Lord? Does the life in His Body come "from the beasts"? Did His Mother "give Him life"? Has He got a soul? Of Christ, the DC says on p. 279: "God created a human life which in the full simplicity of service fulfilled the end of creation. It was the life of his Son, his Image". And that is all, so help me God. *Nothing* about Incarnation, since that involves the creation of His Soul; *nothing* about the role His Mother played in that; *nothing* about His Soul; *nothing* about the Immaculate Conception of His Mother: is any more needed to show how deep seated the rejection of the human soul is lodged in these evolutionists? Since there is a lot they *don't say*, and since they absolutely reject any criticism about what they don't say, we turn our attention on what they *do* say about "soul":

"It was once usual to say that God creates each soul directly each time. But this manner of speaking fails to do justice to two things: one, that creation itself is a reality which strives upwards; and two, that body and soul are not to be divided." (p. 382)

"Up to quite recent times, a solution (to the "problem" of afterlife) was often sought in the simple distinction between "body" and "soul". After death, it was thought, the soul continues to exist separately, while the body perishes. At the Last Judgement, the body is gathered from the clay. This clear picture was an effort to render faithfully the data of the Bible. But an effort must be made to express them otherwise." (p. 473)

"Sometimes Jesus uses the word 'soul'. 'Do not fear those who kill the body but cannot kill the soul' (Mt. 10: 28). But he does not mean to refer to a human spirit which floats free, as it were, of the body. As elsewhere in the Bible, the meaning is rather 'life', 'the living kernel of a man, body and soul'. Our Lord means that there is something of man, that which is most properly himself, which can be saved after death. This 'something' is not the body which is left behind. But Our Lord does not say that this which is truly man is entirely disassociated from a new body. It is not biblical usage to speak of a purely disembodied soul of man. How then are we to understand the texts (referring to the resurrection: 1 Cor. 15: 22; ibid. V. 6; Today you will be with Me in Paradise; 2 Cor. 5: 8)? They speak of a today with reference to something which is not entirely without a body. And at the same time they speak of those who shall live after death. What message is to be read here? It seems to be that we are to think of the 'today' as something that has already begun, and that it is not without the body. In other words, existence after death is already something like the resurrection of the new body. This body of the resurrection is not molecules which are buried and scattered in the earth. Man begins to awake to a new man" (p. 473).

I have quoted these passages at length, so that the many contradictions can be clearly brought to light. I am mainly concerned with the last one.

1. This passage contradicts Christ's teaching. Christ knew the difference between "life" and "soul" and told us so. This passage is private interpretation of Scripture. No evidence is brought out.
2. This passage also contradicts what was stated on p. 470 by the authors: "(In death) Man returns to the earth like an autumn leaf or an animal. Death is radical. Here the deniers of immortality are right. Death is the end of the whole man as we have known him."

    In this passage nothing but a memory remains, in the passage of p. 473 a kernel survives. At least the authors of the DC "know man to have a kernel", so how can they say on p. 470: Death is the end of the whole man *as we know him*; stating on p. 473: as far as they know man, not *the whole man dies* ...

3. p. 470, just quoted, contradicts p. 472: "man is not made to vanish like the beasts".

4. If "soul" means "life" as its true biblical meaning, then we may read the statement on p. 10: "the *soul* of my body comes from the beasts ..."

5. If, however, "soul" means: "surviving kernel" as is also stated here, then the authors have simply shifted the problem: what is the difference between a surviving kernel and a surviving soul?

6. If, according to the long passage above, Christ means by "soul": "life" or "surviving kernel", and this is biblical, then according to the Bible "life in man" and "surviving kernel" are the same. Since the "whole man", according to the DC consists of "life" and "body", and since the "whole man" dies in death, then life and body die; but life, as synonymous with kernel, survives. So life dies and life remains ... And this most confusing and contradictory concoction is the "biblical doctrine on soul" ... According to the DC both the Bible and Christ are confused about soul. If it is not Biblical to speak of a soul which survives after death, and if Christ teaches about a soul which cannot be killed after the body is killed, then either Christ and his teaching are no longer in the Bible, or if Christ's teaching is biblical, then it is "biblical usage" to talk about a surviving soul. Or else Christ did not know His Bible ...

7. If this innermost kernel which is "man most properly him-
    self, even without body and soul and life" **cannot be with-
    out a body and immediately on death takes on another
    body not of molecules,** so that now a **new** man (**not** as we
    know him) exists *already risen today,* then all this is noth-
    ing but a pure contradiction of the Gospel which explicitly
    states "that Christ *rose* on the *third* day". It is even in the
    Credo.

All of a sudden it has become of the utmost significance that
the DC never states that the Risen Christ had reunited with *His*
Body that lay in the grave. Now we know why they need more than
nine pages to explain away the true Resurrection. Christ, according
to the teaching here, **had already immediately resumed another,
unearthly body, not of molecules.** But what happened to His Sacred Body in the grave? In testifying briefly to the empty tomb the
authors then must believe the *lie* that someone else took His Body
..... It is now also of the utmost significance that the DC is completely silent on the fact that **Christ showed His wounds;** that He
asked His disciples **to touch Him** and **to feel His bones.** And finally, to show that His Body was still made up of molecules, He asked
for something **to eat,** and He **ate before their eyes.** St Paul clearly
teaches that "*this* corruptible must take on incorruptibility ..."

Due to its faulty philosophy of man the DC has got itself completely tangled up in a minefield of contradictions, by which reason
and Faith have guarded themselves for over 2000 years. Exactly as
the popes warned us would happen. As far as I am concerned it can
stay there until it blows itself up.

Section B

The Dutch Catechism's Concept of "faith"

Lastly, I must draw attention to a passage in the DC where everything I have stated previously in this essay is wound up in an easy to remember example. Here is the passage on p. 125:

> "There is a level of our being which is deeper than the intellect, more personal than feelings, more human than the subconscious. It is the level on which the two great aspects of our being, knowledge and love, exist. There man's effort to lay hold of truth is inseparable from his striving after goodness. In this primal unity, knowledge is not a cold light and love is not a blind urge. Knowledge is full of love and love itself has vision."

Of this "level of our being" it is stated here: (a) that it is deeper than our intellect, *so intellect is absent there.* (b) It is the level where knowledge and love exist in unity, *so intellect is present there.* It is the level where love has vision, *so intellect extends further than this level*: it extends over love. If love has vision at that level and *there* **knows what it is doing**, and this level is more human than the subconscious, then below the subconscious love knows what it is doing. ... This makes this mysterious totally contradictory and totally unintelligible. The catechism then goes on:

> "It is the level of our being on which we love, where conscience resides."

Here the authors seem to stick to their original assertion that this level is "deeper than the intellect", because it is primarily the level where we love. But conscience has a lot to do with the intellectual act of judgement. Why this unintelligible level is "invented" here comes finally out in the next sentence:

"To this core of our being Jesus addresses himself when demanding faith ... This does not mean that the intellect is excluded or ignored ... And so we come back to describe this central unity with the biblical term belief, that is faith. The word belief is etymologically connected with love."

All this is necessary to explain away the Supernaturality of the act of Divine Faith. It has now become a human act on the human level. And what is more, faith is no longer *an act of the intellect*, but the *name* given to this *unity*, which is a unity on the level where we love, deeper than the intellect, but it does not mean the intellect is excluded or ignored. In other words it is the most crude attempt to introduce into this catechism Teilhard's most fundamental contradiction: the **identity** (be it in some weak opposition) between the natural and the Supernatural in order to have *only one* level: this mysterious unity, to which now is given the name *faith*. The word 'Supernatural' does not even rate a mention in the Topics Index of the DC.

It is this passage where, more than anywhere else, the naked Teilhard doctrine comes to the fore. This description destroys man as he was created by God: as he came from God. Teilhard wanted absolute identity between the natural and the supernatural, or better still: he wanted neither natural nor supernatural: **just one level, one plane, evolution**. Here he got that taught in a catechism. But the penalty for getting it is that the level results in a contradictory entity and so proves its **non-existence**. And so his unity between intellect and will in the absence of the real distinction, and his **identity** of the natural and the supernatural, again in the absence of the real distinction, **become figments of the imagination**. And the dearest, most precious casualty, the one we can least afford to lose, is the most treasured gift of Almighty God to man here on earth: the gift of Supernatural, Divine, Infused Faith. Because this non-existing sameness of the natural order and the Supernatural Order to the one human order, makes every act of faith a natural act of the human intellect, resulting in a **natural faith on the human level**, which completely contradicts Catholic teaching in the gravest of all matters: that of the **Radix** (root) and **Fundamentum** (foundation) of Supernatural life, Sanctification and Sanctifying Grace, Justification and God's inhabitation in the human soul. The Popes were right: tamper with Thomism, then tamper with dogma-thinking it is Thomism, and you end up with **loss of Catholic Faith**.

Book II

The Hidden Schism or The New Catholicism

Frits Albers, Ph.B. (1975)

The first booklet in this series *Teilhard de Chardin and the Dutch Catechism* first appeared in printed form as part of the journal of The International Catholic Priests Association. This was arranged through the good offices of the then Secretary, Rev. John W. Flanagan S.T.L., D.C.L *The Hidden Schism* was published in booklet form also through the efforts of Father Flanagan. The Preface which follows was written by him.

Preface

It is a great honour for me to write the preface of this publication called *The Hidden Schism*, written by one of the ablest Catholic writers of today.

Mr Albers, in this work, goes direct to the root cause of the turmoil in the Church since Vatican II. An Ecumenical Council that was initiated to give new vitality to the Church, has brought instead, disaster and rapid disintegration with great loss of Faith among the sons and daughters of the Church. It is right and natural that investigations should now start to find the cause of this disaster, otherwise the situation will progressively get worse and it will be a "post-mortem" rather than the "kiss of life" which will have to be undertaken.

I have no doubt that Mr Albers has now placed his "axe to the root of the tree", and it is for every Catholic to see that the evils which spring from the designated source, do not continue to thrive in any sphere over which he has authority or influence. Evil will never be conquered by an apathetic approach to it, by those whose duty it is, in justice or in charity to others, to smite it to extinction.

It is worthy of note that the author of this work received, from the *Secretariat of State of the Vatican*, in a letter dated 21st September 1974, "commendation for his theological and philosophical doctrine, which, together with the thanks of the Holy Father, is expressed herewith in the name of His Holiness".

The "theological and philosophical doctrine" commended by the Holy Father, Pope Paul VI, with his gratitude, is for the essay entitled "Teilhard de Chardin and the Dutch Catechism".

If the Pope commends the doctrine of Mr Albers, as contained in the above-mentioned article, and expresses his gratitude for it, obviously, one can rightly conclude that Teilhard de Chardin and the Dutch Catechism, are not approved by the Holy Father. This commendation, moreover, places our author, Mr Albers, in the forefront of Catholic writers.

I have no doubt that this work *The Hidden Schism*, will do much to restore theological sanity and personal sanctity in all who read it and reflect on its contents.

(Rev.) Fr. John W. Flanagan

Preamble

Beginning of the Encyclical Letter
Pascendi Dominici Gregis
On the
Doctrines of the Modernists
His Holiness, Pope St Pius X, 8th September 1907

1. One of the primary obligations assigned by Christ to the office divinely committed to Us of feeding the Lord's flock is that of guarding with the greatest vigilance the deposit of the faith delivered to the saints, rejecting the profane novelties of words and the gainsaying of knowledge falsely so called. There has never been a time when this watchfulness of the supreme pastor was not necessary to the Catholic body, for owing to the efforts of the enemy of the human race, there have never been lacking "men speaking perverse things," (Acts. 20. 30) "vain talkers and seducers," (Tit. 1. 10) "erring and driving into error." (2 Tim. 3. 13) It must, however, be confessed that these latter days have witnessed a notable increase in the number of the enemies of the Cross of Christ, who, by arts entirely new and full of deceit, are striving to destroy the vital energy of the Church, and, as far as in them lies, utterly to subvert the very Kingdom of Christ....

2. That We should act without delay in this matter is made imperative especially by the fact that the partisans of error are to be sought not only among the Church's open enemies; but, what is to be most dreaded and deplored, in her very bosom, and are the

more mischievous the less they keep in the open. We allude, Venerable Brethren, to many who belong to the Catholic laity, and, what is much more sad, to the ranks of the priesthood itself, who, animated by a false zeal for the Church, lacking the solid safeguards of philosophy and theology, nay more, thoroughly imbued with the poisonous doctrines taught by the enemies of the Church, and lost to all sense of modesty, put themselves forward as reformers of the Church; and, forming more boldly into line of attack, assail all that is most sacred in the work of Christ, not sparing even the Person of the Divine Redeemer, whom, with sacrilegious audacity, they degrade to the condition of a simple and ordinary man.

3. Although they express their astonishment that We should number them amongst the enemies of the Church, no one will be reasonably surprised that We should do so, if, leaving out of account the internal disposition of the soul, of which God alone is the Judge, he considers their tenets, their manner of speech, and their action. Nor indeed would he be wrong in regarding them as the most pernicious of all the adversaries of the Church. For, as We have said, they put into operation their designs for her undoing, not from without but from within. Hence, the danger is present almost in the very veins and heart of the Church, whose injury is the more certain from the very fact that their knowledge of her is more intimate. Moreover, they lay the ax not to the branches and shoots, but to the very root, that is, to the faith and its deepest fibers. And once having struck at this root of immortality, they proceed to diffuse poison through the whole tree, so that there is no part of Catholic truth which they leave untouched, none that they do not strive to corrupt. Further, none is more skillful, none more

astute than they, in the employment of a thousand noxious devices; for they play the double part of rationalist and Catholic, and this so craftily that they easily lead the unwary into error; and as audacity is their chief characteristic, there is no conclusion of any kind from which they shrink or which they do not thrust forward with pertinacity and assurance....

4. It is one of the cleverest devices of the Modernists (as they are commonly and rightly called) to present their doctrines without order and systematic arrangement, in a scattered and disjointed manner, so as to make it appear as if their minds were in doubt or hesitation, whereas in reality they are quite fixed and steadfast. For this reason it will be of advantage, Venerable Brethren, to bring their teachings together here into one group, and to point out their interconnection, and thus to pass to an examination of the sources of the errors, and to prescribe remedies for averting the evil results....

Introduction

In a previous essay entitled *Teilhard de Chardin and the Dutch Catechism*, I portrayed in great detail what many consider the central problem in the Catholic Church today: the dissemination of Modernism with its cockle of heresy through the widespread acceptance of the Teilhard de Chardin interpretations of Vatican II to the detriment, as His Holiness Pope St Pius X predicted, to the Catholic Faith of millions: laymen, Priests, Bishops.

Such an article could be viewed as having started "somewhere in the middle" of a very complex, constantly developing process. It is the purpose of this second article:

1. To look back from this somewhat central position to the root-cause of this present-day situation, to study the "how" and "why" of this development.
2. To look ahead and study its fatal, inevitable consequences; consequences which have already come to pass and can be studied from authentic documentations, and ones still to come as logical conclusions.

   It is good, in this context, to be consoled by the parting words of Our Divine Saviour: "I will not relinquish you like orphans". We *can* know. We *are* in a position to understand. We *must* foresee. It is His Will. It is the will of His Vicar as clearly appears from his quoted words.

   From the above the present article divides naturally into two (2) parts. The first part will consist of two (2) chapters:

(a) a study of the long preparation towards the Teilhard de Chardin brand of Modernism; and

(b) an even more important study of the careful preparation towards its acceptance.

These two aspects are *not* the same and must *not* be confused. The second part too will consist of two (2) chapters:

(c) a study of the consequences of the acceptance of the Teilhard doctrine as it affected a particular diocese: its catechetics, the training of its priests and related topics; and

(d) a study of what may logically be expected to happen if these disastrous effects are allowed to develop to their inevitable outcomes, given the present situation and taking into account the forces that are working towards a definite end.

To understand all this even better it is necessary not only to look back and to look ahead, but also to branch out sideways and study a parallel situation which is rapidly developing in the secular society of our times. This parallel development will be the subject-matter of a Third Article, which will enable us to follow more accurately the *combined* trend of things to their logical conclusions.

I cannot stress enough, as I have done in previous articles, the *absolute* necessity for a Catholic, to understand, to *know*, what is meant by CATHOLIC FAITH. In order to keep a deep love for this priceless possession, a Catholic must know what it is, and how it is different from any other faith. We just read the warning of Pope St

Pius X: that the axe is being laid at the very root, that is to the Faith itself, and we will hear Teilhard proclaim that such is his very intention.

Part I

The long preparation towards the Teilhard de Chardin brand of Modernism

Modernism is the general name given to the school of thought, or system, which puts the fundamental truths of the Catholic Faith in jeopardy by its constant effort to subject the whole of Catholic doctrine to the requirements of human thought. Whatever the exponent of "human thought" may be at a particular time. In its early days it was Rationalist philosophy (Diderot, d'Alembert, Voltaire), then Positivism, Science, and finally, in its present day virulent Teilhard de Chardin form, the whole of Catholic Dogma must be subjected to the requirements of that pseudo-science: Evolution. The immediate aim of Modernism is the total destruction and collapse of Catholic Faith. Its ultimate aim is the domination of the Catholic Church by the Prince of Darkness. Aspects which make Modernism more understandable are Naturalism (Rousseau) and Humanism.

To give you an idea of what is meant here: Just imagine what would happen to those glorious dogmas of the Catholic Faith such as the Divinity of Christ, the perpetual Virginity of Mary, the Divine Maternity of Mary, the Inerrancy of Scripture, if they could only be accepted in so far as science with its "proofs" and "disproofs" would have the final say in it. What would be left of the most fundamental doctrine of them all: the blessed Trinity?

Right from the start of this dissertation two things must be clearly borne in mind:

(i) The absolute impossibility of the Catholic Church ever being overpowered by the forces of darkness, no matter how reduced and almost invisible the Church may become; and

(ii) The utter possibility of whole sections, even very large sections of Catholics losing their Catholic Faith to Modernism and thus no longer constituting the Catholic Church, no matter how perplexingly big and well-organized their world-wide body may appear to us.

It must further be recognized that it is one thing to prepare a world-wide system of heresy and quite another to have it accepted. The former has received quite a covering in responsible books and publications. The latter is subtle, is the more pernicious (as the Holy Father called it), has not been adequately dealt with, but has caused the wide-spread damage. Adam and Eve were both tempted to the *same* act of disobedience, but they were subjected to *different preparations of acceptance*. The preparation towards the *acceptance* of a new faith is just as important as the preparation of the new faith itself.

Chapter One

A Short History of Modernism and Its Transition into Teilhard's System

How far the cancer of Modernism has eaten into the very life of many Catholics becomes immediately apparent to anyone who takes time off to read what Popes and Councils of the Church have said over the last 140 years. An excellent compendium of the history of Modernism and its errors and heresies is contained in a recent book: *The Enemy within the Gate*, by Fr. John McKee. The book, however good on the Modernism condemned by Pope St Pius X, is comparatively silent on the transition, vital to us, to the Modernism of Teilhard which has swept the Church in our times.

To give you an idea how far back one has to go to hear a clear echo on the difficulties of our time, I quote the following entry from Herder's Church Lexicon:

"Clement August Von Droste-Vischering ... became Archbishop of Cologne in 1835 ... His condemnation of writings favouring heretical tendencies and his disavowal of *certain professors of theology infected by heresy*, aroused the animosity of the government against him ... After an imprisonment of two years, the Archbishop was honourably released. He resigned his position as Archbishop of Cologne and went to Rome where he became advisor to Pope Gregory XVI."

It was this Pope who in 1835 condemned the works of one of those German theology professors, one Fr. George Hermes, as heretical for exactly the same reasons: positivism, as Modernism would be condemned more than 70 years later in 1907, by Pope St Pius X. From 1832 onwards the uninterrupted stream of condemnations from the Holy See, gaining in clarity as the infernal intentions of the enemy became more clear, did not leave anyone who valued his Catholic Faith in any doubt as to the dividing line between Science and Revelation.

Most of this is available to any alert Catholic, even today, but maybe only a Saint like Pope Pius X could foresee the unprecedented upheavals in the Church of the second half of the twentieth century and the ferocity with which the *break* with the past would come. For if most of us are conscious of one thing, it is *not* that we developed from a bad situation before Vatican II to a worse situation afterwards, but rather, that such an awful lot of people who still seem to be inside the Church, appear to have *broken* with the past and with tradition. On the one hand, the devil and his minions *gradually* developed the successful (let us call it) school of Modernism, condemned by *Pascendi*, into the highly successful system of Modernism of Teilhard, condemned by *Humani Generis* of 1950.

But next to this gradual development of this new faith something else developed. And it was in this area that at a given instant something gave, something collapsed, and this is what I have called the top-secret, very elusive and subtle preparation towards the *acceptance* of the Modernistic thought, of the deceit. Many Catholics have become Modernistic *not* because of intellectual conviction (they would hardly know how to formulate it), but for totally different reasons with which we will occupy ourselves in the second chapter.

First: how did the Modernism of Loisy and Tyrell develop into the Modernism of Teilhard de Chardin? How did it go from a "school" into a closely knitted "system"? Let us listen to the ones appointed by God to teach us in these matters.

I return to Pope St Pius X and quote the paragraph in *Pascendi* immediately following the opening paragraphs of the Encyclical quoted above in the Preamble to this essay.

> "To proceed in an orderly manner in this somewhat ab-
> struse subject, it must first of all be noted that the Modernist
> sustains and includes within himself a *manifold personality*; he
> is a philosopher, a believer, a theologian, an historian, a critic,
> an apologist, a reformer."

This is a clear description of the various strands of their school. In this lengthy Encyclical the Holy Father deals with each strand separately in amazing depth.

Now let us listen to the words with which another Pope, Pius XII, introduces the body of his argument in his equally famous Encyclical *Humani Generis* of 1950.

> "A glance at the world outside the Catholic fold will famil-
> iarize us easily enough with the false directions which the
> thought of the learned often take. Some (he means *inter alia*
> Teilhard here) will contend that the Theory of Evolution as it is
> called – a theory which has <u>not yet been proved beyond con-</u>

<u>tradiction even in the sphere of natural science</u> – <u>applies to the origin of all things whatsoever</u> ... *These false evolutionary notions*, with their denial of all that is fixed or abiding in human experience (tradition) <u>have paved the way for a new philosophy of error.*"*

So, in the intervening forty-three years separating these two great Encyclicals, what consisted of various strands had now developed into a modernistic system: evolution, which system proved to be just as fallacious as the strands from which it was composed and out of which it had grown.

It is from the central point of "these false evolutionary notions" that everything in Catholic dogma, Catholic Bible exegesis, Catechetics and Tradition is being viewed and taught by disobedient sons and daughters of the Church. Pope St Pius X clearly showed that no human system, however sound, can on its own ever be the touchstone of Revelation and Faith. What then about the driftsand of the theory of evolution, which is in the process of being discarded by an ever widening circle of scientists on purely scientific grounds?

That Evolution was chosen by the enemies of God to become the vehicle for introducing systematic Modernism within the Catholic Church on a grand scale in order to subvert it more effectively from *within*, is borne out by numerous testimonies. The very possibility of this happening did not escape clear-sighted men in Darwin's own lifetime. Professor Sedgwick of Cambridge, a good friend of Darwin, read *Origin of Species* and then wrote to Darwin, Christmas 1859, warning him that, if his evolutionary teachings

were accepted "humanity would suffer a damage that might brutal-
ize it and sink the human race into a lower state of degradation
than any into which is has fallen since written records".

The following two quotes are from an interesting book called
Darwin, Before and After by Robert E. D. Clark, M.A. Ph.D.

> "Evolution, in short, gave the doer of evil a respite from his
> conscience. The most unscrupulous behaviour towards a com-
> petitor could now be rationalized. Evil could be called good.
>
> "In time, the theory of evolution permeated human thought
> in almost every direction. The ultimate result was exactly what
> Sedgwick had said would happen: brutalization. The new doc-
> trine very soon began to undermine religion."

Books have been written, too many even to enumerate, about
how the theory of evolution has inspired Big Business, Education,
Prussianism, Communism, Fascism, Religion (only so called, like
the Dutch Catechism, p. 10: "the life in my body comes from the
beasts"), Irreligion, Sex philosophy, Abortion, Society. On the last
topic, B.G. Sandhurst wrote the book *How Heathen is Britain?*
(1948), from which the following passage is quoted in the discussion of Army Officer trainees: "Often one-third of my audiences
are so conditioned by the theory of evolution that they cannot believe that they are in any way different from the other animals".

How scientific is all this? The position in this regard is very well
summed up by the following quote from *The Premises of Evolutionary Thought* by R.J. Rushdoony:

"Sigmund Freud, as an evolutionary scientist, has been a source of embarrassment to his many dedicated followers at one critical point: Freud grounded his evolutionary thinking firmly on the theories of Lamarck. The inheritance of acquired characteristics is basic to Freud's anthropology, biology, psychology. In the face of extensive criticism Freud 'adhered throughout his life to the Lamarckian belief' (Jones). At this point even his devoted disciple and biographer Dr Ernest Jones, criticized Freud as 'What one must call an obstinate adherent of this discredited Lamarckism'. Freud, however, was resolute. *Because of his hostility to religion* the doctrine of Evolution was intensely important to Freud, and evolutionary theory provided for no effective mechanism for evolution apart from Lamarck. *To deny Lamarck* and the inheritance of acquired characteristics was to posit a god-like power somewhere in or behind evolution and to introduce illegitimately and element resembling the supernatural."

Multiply this incident a million times over and over again: the blind acceptance of unscientific wishful thinking against evidence, in order to vent one's spleen against God, Religion the Supernatural, the Church, and one can appreciate the picture of the Catholic Church, surrounded by scientific hostility, as a beleaguered City of God. In order to see this even better, see *The Twilight of Evolution* by H. Morris, pp 25-26, for religious hostility; and *Scientific Studies in Special Creation* (Lammerts), pp 338-343, for social and educational hostility since all hostilities have been drenched with evolutionary theory, "those false evolutionary notions ...".

What about erosions caused by evolution within the beleaguered city? Here, for sake of space only, we must confine ourselves to the writings of the late Pierre Teilhard de Chardin, who, as we will see, deliberately chose to remain within the visible confines of the Catholic Church, the beleaguered city, in order to be better able to subvert her from within. However, it is practically impossible to quote any other modern Modernist who has raised his voice against the Church from within, who was not deeply influenced by Teilhard. Even if they do not follow his absurd system, they have adopted his principles and have all clamoured for recognition of evolution as a legitimate theological principle to explain Bible and Dogma. Here is an example from the writings of one of those theologians of repute, Fr. Karl Rahner S.J.

"In the present state of theology and science it cannot be proved that polygenism conflicts with orthodox teaching on Original Sin. *It would be better, therefore, if the Magisterium refrained from censuring polygenism.*"

In *Original Sin in the Light of Modern Science*, the late Fr. Patrick O'Connell. B.D., demolished Rahner's preposterous claim.

Returning then to Teilhard we have reached a critical stage in our discourse. Enough is known about his theories, but what about his intent? Was he simply mistaken or a dupe, or was there more to it? Here we can start to see a glimmer of the naked face of Satan himself in his twofold preparation. Teilhard was certainly used to introduce a deceitful system into the Church and he knew what he was doing. But was he also used deliberately to have the system *ac-*

cepted? If the latter is true then Teilhard is just as indispensible as he is inexcusable with regard to the damage done, even if, after the deadly poison has taken effect, many now pretend that they have discarded him as a useless syringe. I am sorry if we only have used the highlights in the history of Modernism to come to this position, but the detailed study of what is to follow is imperative if one wants to keep a clear head and untroubled eye in the massive confusion all around us. We will finish this chapter with an outline of Teilhard's position and use it as an introduction to the second chapter where we study the widespread acceptance of his subversion and the underlying causes.

Teilhard's brand of evolution is best described as *theistic pantheism*, which of course is a contradiction in terms and therefore non-existent. Do not think for one moment that the disobedient sons and daughters of the Church who pored over his works and propagated them, ever came across a definition as simple as the one I just used. First-class minds have come to this conclusion and we can verify the truth of their findings. But like always in God's Church: in the early stages it was simply a question *of obeying those* to whom more light and enlightenment was given for the care of souls entrusted to them. After the initial obedience the Light would then gradually be communicated to all those "who had done God's will on earth as it was done (and known) in Heaven". But they who had disregarded the strong words of Pope St Pius X in *Pascendi* and *Lamentabili* and who had accepted the principles of Modernism, saw no cause for concern when Modernism gradually got dressed up as evolution, and they were stiffened in their hostility to the Magisterium when this "misunderstood genius" was trying to put some theism into evolution. That was good enough for them. That it was pantheism either escaped them or they did not believe it. Wasn't evolution proved by science? Then it must be full of God if it came from God, ran their arguments. But let us listen a bit more than they did to the man himself.

"My spirit has always been naturally pantheistic. I felt its inborn *and unconquerable aspirations*, but I dare not give them free reign because I could not reconcile them with my faith. But after these experiences and others like them I have found a life-long and unalterable peace. I live in the heart of a single element, the centre of cosmic power." (*Hymn of the Universe*)

"I am essentially pantheistic in my thinking and pantheistic by temperament, and my whole life has been spent in proclaiming that there is a true pantheism of union." (Duggan in *Teilhardism and the Faith*)

Miss Hilda Graef, in her book, *Mystics of our Time* (she places Teilhard amongst the mystics), relates that he as a child of six had a bar of iron hidden which he used to bring out from time to time to "adore". He would hold it up and say: "God. Iron." And that his commentary on this childish habit, sixty years later, was: "In this instinctive movement which made me truly worship a small piece of metal, there was a strong sense of self-giving ... and my spiritual life has been merely *a development of this*."

Fr. North S.J., and others, confirm Miss Graef's account of young Teilhard adoring pieces of metal – Fr. Leroy S.J. mentions a spanner – and adds that Teilhard's mother would take the spanner off him and try to substitute devotion to the Sacred Heart instead. Fr. Duggan sums it all up rather well with a quote from Teilhard:

"The divine and created, natural and supernatural, are *organically* all of one piece."

So, whatever his system is going to be, it is obvious that it is based, as far as the Catholic Church is concerned, on a totally unacceptable idea. Well, he calls his system *evolution* and, while accepting the scientific "findings", he tried to show that evolution had a *within*. This was, as we saw, totally rejected by Freud and was to be rejected by all outsiders as we will see. The trouble for Teilhard now is that with this "within", his system not only did not become Catholic or even Christian: *it became doubly objectionable.*

"Evolution is not just hypotheses or theories: it is a general condition to which all theories, all hypotheses, all systems must bow and which they must satisfy if they are thinkable and true ..."

So says Teilhard, and then sets out to "prove" it. That he was not very convincing in this becomes apparent when one is confronted with the following quote from Prof. Gaylord Simpson of Harvard University:

"Teilhard's beliefs as to the course and causes of evolution are *not* scientifically acceptable because they are not based on scientific premises."

Why is this condemnation so remarkable? Not only was Prof. Simpson an extreme evolutionist, but he was made by Teilhard one of the executors of his literary will, and so Simpson would have defended Teilhard if he could have done so without loss of his own reputation. Teilhard's brand of evolution did not fool outsiders like Simpson: it was strictly for disobedient Catholics. Can this be proved? Can it be shown to be anti-Catholic.

Teilhard was well aware that his groping for a solution satisfactory to him must be within a new system. He was equally well aware of the consequences:

"A collective optimism, realistic and courageous, must definitely replace the pessimism and individualism, whose overgrown notions of sin and personal salvation have gradually burdened and *perverted* the Christian spirit. Let us then acknowledge the situation honestly: not only the 'Imitation of Christ' but also the *Gospel itself needs to undergo this correction, and the whole world will make them undergo it.*" (1929)

"What increasingly dominates my interest is the effort to establish within myself and to diffuse around me a *new religion* in which the personal God is no longer the great Neolithic landowner of times gone by, but the *soul* of the world, as the

cultural and religious stage we have reached now demands."
(1936)

"I have come to the conclusion that, in order to pay for a
drastic valorization and amortization of the substance of
things, *a whole series of re-shaping of certain representations or
attitudes, which seem to us definitely fixed by Catholic dogma,
has become necessary,* if we sincerely wish to Christify Evolution. Seen thus, and because of an ineluctable necessity, one
could say that a *hitherto unknown form of religion* is gradually
germinating in the heart of modern man in the furrow opened
by the idea of evolution." (1953)

The following is taken from a letter to an ex-priest who had left
the Church, and after noticing that the Encyclical *Humani Generis*
was written in condemnation of Teilhard's ideas, wrote him a letter
inviting Teilhard to join him in his battle to change the Church
from without. Here is the body of Teilhard's reply to the ex-priest.

"Basically I consider – as you do – that the Church reaches
a period of mutation or necessary reformation. To be more
precise: I consider that the reformation in question (and a
much more profound one than the sixteenth century) is no
longer a matter of institutions and ethics, but of Faith. Having
stated my views I cannot see any better means of bringing
about what I anticipate than to work towards this reform from
within. In the course of the last fifty years I have watched the
revitalization of Catholic thought and life taking place around
me – *in spite of the encyclicals* – too closely not to have un-

bounded confidence in the ability of the old Roman stem to re-vivify itself. Let us then each work in our separate sphere: all upward movements converge."

To me and many with me, these are the words and intentions of a heretic. This is not poetic licence: these are the systematic actions of a man who knows what he is about "to lay the ax not to the branches and shoots, but to the very root, that is, to the faith and its deepest fibers" as was predicted would happen by a Pope and Saint more than 40 years previously in *Pascendi.*

That the enemies of the Church understood perfectly well what Teilhard was doing here, will come out further on in this article. And just as Freud needed an unscientific system of evolution in order to cling to his antipathy against God and Religion, so many Catholics are clinging to Teilhardism in their hostility for and "old fashioned" Catholic Church and in their hope to change Her to their own liking.

For further reading on this matter, see Fr O'Connell, *op. cit.,* pp. 58-59.

Chapter Two

The Careful Preparation towards
the Acceptance of Teilhard's System

You can lead a horse to water, but you cannot make him drink. If planning a world-wide, comprehensive and subtle heresy is one thing, then its acceptance needs a different preparation. A heresy does not necessarily recommend itself on its intellectual content. It is absolutely impossible that heresy will ever be embraced in the Supernatural Light of Catholic Faith, which is the Light of God Himself, communicated here on earth to the human mind as a free gift from God to believe all that God has revealed and the holy Catholic Church proposes to us for our consent as having been re-vealed by God. We have God's guarantee that neither the Catholic Church nor Holy Scripture will ever propose heresy to us to be be-lieved. Only a mere human faith can accept heresy, but in doing so will darken and eventually extinguish the Supernatural Light of Faith and plunge the mind into darkness. And so it is in darkness of mind only, by the feeble torch light of reason alone, that Teil-hard's system seems to fit the answers. If that is so, then the big question is: "*Who turned the light of Faith off?*" The answer to that question is being examined in this chapter.

In the speech given by the Grand Master, Jacques Mitterrand, at the occasion of the General Assembly of the Grand Orient of France, held in Paris from 3rd to 7th September 1962, in which speech French Freemasonry claimed Teilhard de Chardin as their own, Mitterrand made an overt reference to the 18th Rule of the Kabbala, the tenth century top secret mystical doctrine of a Jewish forerunner of the Freemasons, which states:

> "Beware that you do not dish up to the Christian dogs their deadly strychnine pill plain, but be sure to wrap it up in a large slice of soft flesh."

Satan wanted desperately for the Catholic defenders of the beleaguered City of God to accept Teilhard's *New Religion* so that they would lose their Catholic Faith and so become displaced persons in their own concentration camp. He knew that many – especially among the Clergy – for reasons we will discuss shortly, had already *pro foro interno*, i.e. in their own private thoughts, placed many secret question marks against not a few doctrines and practices of the Catholic Faith. But to go from private doubts to the wholesale jettisoning of Catholic dogma as required by Teilhard for the embrace of evolution, is too much to ask, unless this embrace of the world and the flesh can be made "holy". And in evolution, no matter how unscientific, this embrace of the world and the flesh is made to appear holy to meet the *soul* of evolution, Teilhard's new "personal god".

And so, when Vatican II, under the direct inspiration from God (as is so often the case) to reveal once again the secret thoughts of many, opened a window of compassion on the world, millions of Catholics, well prepared by Teilhard's aberrations and deaf to the warnings of the Church, took this as their signal that

God had sanctioned this man's call to the world, and out they flocked to its embrace.

The whole beleaguering, after all, proved to be nothing more than a terrible nightmare: did not both camps meet over this inspired evolution, and did they not all share a common faith in this precious evolution? The whole ghastly mistake of the past: *Trent, Vatican I, Pascendi, Humani Generis*, better be forgotten, the quicker the better. Teilhard's improved Christianity, built on his precious evolution, was the religion of the future; a Christianity which will allow you to follow your own conscience, to have the pill, abortions, freemasonry, communism: all in the name of evolution, an evolution which calls sin nothing more startling than a mistake.

The constant hammering from the intellectual world outside the Catholic Church: that the Church is wrong, that the Church is fighting a desperate rearguard action against the findings of science and evolution, making educated Catholics like Charlesworth more and more embarrassed and ill at ease, has at last had its effect. And the condemnation of this Jesuit-Priest-Evolutionist-poet Mystic Teilhard de Chardin was just about the last straw. His synthesis embracing all: science, "dogma", world, god, was precisely what everybody had been looking for. This blue-print of things to come *simply couldn't be wrong*. The people outside the Church were right: there was something seriously wrong with the Church. It badly needed updating. What better chance than interpreting Vatican II in the light of the teachings of this genius, this second "Thomas Aquinas"?

But then, after the first exhilaration had died down, something totally unexpected started to happen: slowly at first, but unmistakably as time went on: the various crises of identity arose. Priests all of a sudden found themselves in the wrong camp. Surely, on the teachings of this man, celibacy should be optional! Didn't the whole Church go over then to this new religion with its newly found freedom?

Modernistic bishops, Teilhardian religious, free-wheeling Catholics: all had the greatest difficulty in recognizing their new surroundings. The "new catechetics" did not seem to make sense or fit in with the old one. Poverty, chastity, obedience all looked so hopelessly outmoded, so incongruous in the embrace of a world in evolution. And so one could go on and list sign after sign that the global exodus from the Catholic Church has created a vast camp of displaced persons who have lost their identity, their freedom and their Faith.

They are living in make-shift hovels, without the Sacrifice, without Mary, without the Rosary, but because there are so many of them they are convinced that they are the Catholic Church and that they have the right to impose their views on the old reactionaries, the not-with-it people who preferred to stay in their Father's House. But why didn't it work? It ought to have worked! It looked so much like the real thing. *There was only one thing wrong with it: the Church had forbidden it*. But surely ...

There was a precedence for this. Just as all the misery, all the dreadful sins, all the death and wars in the world came into this world through the *One Sin* of our first parents: *Original Sin of disobedience*, so the rebellion, the apostasy, the confusion, the heresies, the disobedience to the Magisterium, the broken unity, the general paralysis and the crises of identity *all* have their origin in the *one single act*: the almost universal acceptance of Teilhard's obliteration of the first Original Sin in order to make a breach for his unscientific evolution. And into the breach came every conceivable evil except evolution ...

Here then is part of the gloating speech by Grandmaster Mitterrand, not only to the assembly of French Freemasons, but over their heads to the whole world:

"By contrast to us Freemasons, the Catholics, in name of ecumenism, do not hold fast to their past in order to learn from it; they rather do all they can to disown their Tradition in order to tailor their religion to renewal. Now why should this happen? Well, pay attention to this, that you may learn how all this took its beginning.

One day a scientist rose from their ranks, a genuine scientist, Pierre Teilhard de Chardin. Maybe without full realization, he committed Lucifer's crime, which the Church of Rome has so often accused us Freemasons of perpetrating: he declared that in the phenomenon of hominization, or, to use Teilhard's own formula, in the Noosphere, that is the sum-total or mass of collective consciences surrounding the globe like the lowest layer of the atmosphere *it is man and not God* who ranks first and is the chief architect of the process. When this collective consciousness has reached its apogee, at the Omega-point as Teilhard himself would put it, then we will have produced the new type of man as we wish him to be: *free in his flesh*, untrammelled in his mind. Teilhard thus put man on the altar and since he adored man he could no longer adore God.

Rome grasped it accurately, and through all the backward powers, concentrated in its bosom *it condemned Teilhard* and prohibited the publication of his works.

But what has been the use of this condemnation, you will ask me. Did it benefit Rome? Did it not much more benefit Teilhard? Listen carefully. During his life Teilhard could not publish any of his texts. Only after his death became it possible to bring his books out through the Editions de Seuil and Grasset, obviously without the blessing of the Church. Imagine that we had found ourselves in such a country as Spain where the Church controls everything: neither Editions de Seuil nor Grasset would have had a chance of publishing Teilhard de Chardin's work. Ah! There they all are, then, all and each in their successive refusals to acknowledge his works, trying to preserve *by brute force* all the powers of the past in order to *crush the future.*

And so it is left to us and to our mission to serve the future. Not satisfied by being – at home and in our temples – the secret republic (i.e. the real power behind the State), *we are at the same time and much more* **the counter-church** (*sic*), because we are the men of life, the men of hope, of light, of progress, of intelligence and reason."

And then Jacques Mitterrand took the blasphemy even further by identifying Freemasonry with *the truth*, and *the light*: the source of *all truth and of all light* ... (*Das Zeichen Mariens*, Oct. Nov. Dec. 1971, Vol V. Nos 6, 7, 8).

So these are the people who have taken Teilhard under their wing, avowing to continue his work while gloating over the fact that in total disobedience to the Magisterium his works are being published, blessing themselves that it did not happen in Spain; and apparently approving of Teilhard's mortal sin of disobedience of making a will bequeathing all his property to atheistic executors, so that his works posthumously can be published outside the jurisdiction of the Church. Only totally subverted Teilhard de Chardin "Catholics" could clamour to the Holy Father to lift the ban on Freemasonry so that our Holy Mother the Church, the Spotless Bride of the Lamb of God, could "benefit" from the invasion by this "counter-church".

But that is not all: Teilhard was not only in all secrecy a member of the Freemasons himself, he was a member of the ultra-subvertive sect, the Martinists, who for two hundred years had worked unceasingly for the day that the "Christian dogs" would take the bait of the whole agglomerate of syncretism, gnostic Rosicrucian mumbo-jumbo and pseudo-scientific clap-trap and swallow the deadly strychnine.

The unprecedented scale of defection to this new church of darkness by so many priests and laypeople in our days makes it virtually impossible to suppress the suspicion that, like in the days of the Arian heresy, the bishops collectively are involved, i.e. the bishops as a body, with the good ones the exceptions. What is the truth here? The truth here is that the college of bishops is just as deeply split and divided as the rest of the Church and that they are reaping the thorny harvest of more than one hundred years basking in the false sun of liberalism by so many of them. For precedence I refer to an excellent article "Cardinal Newman and the Authority in the Church" by Mgr. Flanagan, an *Approaches* supplement, which would serve as an introduction.

For the contemporary problem we could do worse than listen very carefully to the words of the late Most Rev. William Adrian, Bishop of Nashville, Tennessee. This prelate wrote a penetrating article on this very subject, entitled *How did it all Happen?*, which began as follows:

"Ever since the Second Vatican Council I have been puzzled to know what caused the sudden outbreak of mass confusion and heartache that is affecting our Catholic people of America today – even to the extent of serious rebellion against Church authority and many defections. In all my life I have witnessed nothing, nothing remotely approaching this turmoil that is so deeply affecting all Catholics – Bishops, Priests, Religious, and the laity. The UPI calls this the most startling ferment of centuries in the Church.

Even the non-Catholic has been taken by surprise. Dr. Martin Marty, a Lutheran theologian, recently wrote:

'The Roman Catholic renewal has been beset by fickle theology, simplistic thinking, thoughtlessness and a frequent compulsion to leave the rocking ship. Catholic theologians have been offering experiments as solutions, and tentative steps as the last word. *They listen not to all the thousands of years of re-*

ligious wisdom before them: they talk but they have *nothing to say...'*

But how did so many of our Catholic clergy so suddenly get this way? The dramatic story really begins one hundred years ago with the summoning of the First Vatican Council by Pope Pius IX ..."

Bishop Adrian then goes on in some detail to show that the Dogma of the Infallibility of the Pope as defined by that Council, was ill received, at least *in foro interno* (in their private thoughts and convictions) by many Northern European Bishops. To rationalize their attitude they saw in it a barb of perpetuating Italian dominance over the Church and over the Papacy, and so the whole dispute degenerated into one of political factions and alliances. More at home in politics than in following their Saviour on the *Via Dolorsa* in search of the lost sheep, these by and large wealthy bishops could afford the luxury of listening to the political arguments of their liberal theologians who introduced them to ways of thinking completely alien to the Redeemer's Gospel: evolution of Dogma, power sharing through collegiality, de-institutionalizing the powerful "Church of Rome". As so often in the Church: the very first nurturing of a doubt in the wisdom of the Holy Spirit and the harbouring of thoughts "that God could have ulterior motives" for demanding obedience, even from Bishops (for Catholics such a powerful re-enactment of the first temptation in paradise), forced these Bishops to start walking roads which they did not really want to pursue, but from which they could no longer extricate themselves without loss of face with their less scrupulous contemporaries.

And so the Light must have gradually dimmed in these leaders of the Faith in Europe and they relied increasingly more heavily on the artificial light of reason, science and social studies to find their way, readily supplied (as Bishop Adrian tells us) by such "luminaries" as Kung, Davis, Rahner, Schillebeeckx, Congar, Baum, and a few others, such as Schoonenberg, who wrote the *Dutch Catechism* and was able to "sell it" to the Hierarchy. Recognize them? *All* were *periti* at the Second Vatican Council. At the Council the Bishops these *periti* had introduced to their thinking were at a (dubious) advantage of being articulate in the modern philosophy and theology built on Teilhard's ideas and the need was felt by other Bishops to become "updated".

Through private lectures and crash-courses (IDOC) these *periti* received an influence far greater than their worth. Before the Second Vatican Council these *periti* were considered by many as extremists, but National Hierarchies could not now all of a sudden disown them, now that they were so much in demand by other Bishops.

As is so often the case: God creates a situation (as the Holy Man Simeon explained to us in the Temple) "which reveals (in fact: forces open) the secret thoughts in the hearts of many". Spurred on by their skilful *periti*, Vatican II, (which for the Holy Father and the Church in union with him, became a perfectly legitimate means of reviewing the Church's position), became for the liberal Bishops on both sides of the Atlantic, the fierce battleground for *collegiality*.

Listen once more to Bishop Adrian:

"The *main issue* at the Second Vatican Council was that of collegiality – or the question of how the bishops, as a body, could somehow rule over the Church, the Pope holding only a primacy of honour, not of jurisdiction independent of the bishops. The liberal bishops knew that, in order to destroy the autocratic power of the Pope and the Curia, they had to stress the idea of rule by the bishops collectively, and that they could over-rule the Pope. Also, such a move would overcome the embarrassing doctrine of Papal Infallibility so inimical to non-Catholics."

But the Pope intervened and corrected the false doctrines created by the bishops, which later drew from Hans Kung the bitter comment: "The Pope has an exaggerated view of his office. The papacy, after all is said and done, is a human institution and has no origin in the Gospels." So what happened next? Let us hear Bishop Adrian once more:

"These liberal theologians seized on the Council as the *means of de-Catholicizing the Catholic Church while pretending only to de-Romanize it.* As the council developed some of the originally somnolent American bishops, catching fire from their alert European colleagues, became the able engineers of liberal proposals, going beyond the Europeans in ferocious, vituperative attacks on the Roma Curia. Yet, however brilliant the American *periti* may have been, they got their ideas from the European Catholic liberal theologians and bishops. These European *periti* who really *imposed their theories* upon the

Council Fathers were themselves *deeply imbued with the errors of Teilhardism and Situation Ethics*, which errors *ultimately destroy all divine faith and morality, and all constituted authority.* They make the person the centre and judge of all truth and morality irrespective of what the Church teaches. Herein lies the *root* of the modern evil."

Conclusion

This conclusion of Part I serves as an Introduction to Part II, in which we will analyse the actual state of a diocese after it was exposed to cyclone Teilhard, and what this means for the future.

Many minds poisoned by Teilhardism, Modernism and Marxism were present during the deliberations of Vatican II. But during the sessions of the Council these minds were powerless against the direct protection from heresy, given by the Holy Spirit to the Catholic Church-in-session in union with Her head, the Vicar of Christ on earth. The Holy Spirit used their minds too, to formulate what He wanted, not what they wanted. But what proved impossible during Vatican II: that the Catholic Church would be handed over to her enemies, became for the greater part a reality, when *Her enemies got hold of the interpretations of Vatican II, determined to change Her after all.*

The evil Teilhardism, as we saw, did not just happen overnight: it was carefully planned. But it hit an indifferent humanity, a group of Catholic Bishops, prelates, priests and lay intellectuals: all weakened by the same dissatisfaction with the Catholic Church, and by their loss of faith in Her. *They wanted Her changed. And overnight*

Teilhardism became the blue-print they had been looking for: to change the Church after their own ideas and fancies.

The First Sin committed in Paradise, as we learned in the Catechism, darkened the human intellect. This is totally unacceptable to a Modernist, so it can't be true ... This light was abundantly restored by Christ's Redemption in the Light of the Supernatural, Divine Virtue of Catholic Faith. But this second "Original Sin", committed by the West on the teachings of Teilhard: the sin of relegating the First Sin to the realm of *myths*, has darkened again the minds of Bishops, Priests and Religious, and what many Catholic see as abominable in the Light of their Catholic Faith: Teilhardism, became to all who lost this Supernatural Light, a blue-print for renewal, but a renewal *not* inspired by God, but seen in the torchlight of human thought.

The division between these two groups is the *hidden schism* which runs right through every diocese on earth, every parish, every convent, every presbytery, every seminary and probably every household. "There will be two people ostensibly doing the same thing", says Our Lord, "one will be accepted, the other will be rejected".

What this means will be analysed in greater detail in Part II.

Part II

The Fatal Consequences of this Hidden Schism

This Part II will consist of two chapters. Chapter Three will deal with consequences which have already taken place in time: facts resulting from the hidden schism caused by the factors studied in the first two chapters. These facts can be verified by anyone who has access to the normal sources of information. Since I live in the Archdiocese of Melbourne, Australia, I can only deal with the situation as it developed here.

The final chapter (chapter four) of this paper is a view of the future. In that chapter I will discuss what may logically be expected to happen given the situation as it exists today and given the forces that are working towards very definite ends.

Chapter Three

The post-Vatican II Development
of the Archdiocese of Melbourne
under Archbishop Knox

We begin this chapter by listening again to Bishop W. Adrian of Nashville, Tennessee.

"These European revolutionists, already during the sessions of Vatican II and more so after, flooded this nation with their propaganda. Many of them, like Hans Kung, Karl Rahner, Charles Davis, Schillebeeckx, Baum, Congar appeared in person in America on the invitation of some bishop or 'educator.'

They wrote and distributed books and articles, they invaded our colleges and seminaries, even Catholic schools. Their propaganda was further abetted by the establishment-controlled liberal Catholic press by sensational slanted reporting.

Finally, a factor largely contributing to this revolutionary movement in the Church has been the silence and timidity of those whose grave duty is to call a halt to these anti-Catholic movements within the Church, chiefly the bishops.

And yet, Pope Paul again and again admonished the bishops of the world to take a rigorous, courageous stand in preventing the spread of these abuses. But the voice of the Holy Father has remained almost alone in proclaiming the truths of the Catholic Church, in condemning the audacious voices of the schismatics, the heretics, the secularists, and the deploring widespread flaunting of constituted authority. The do-nothing attitude of those in authority is greeted with satisfaction by revolutionists and reformers alike, and every day they are becoming more brazen in declaring with dictatorial voice '*that they alone are interpreting with understanding the Spirit of Vatican II*', whereas in fact they are distorting and disobeying its decrees.

Even more, some liberal bishops are not only permitting but encouraging, *even to giving orders*, flagrant disregard for some of the teaching of the Magisterium of the Church and the Decrees of Vatican II. Since these radicals were stopped in the Council in their attempt to gain more power, by the authoritative voice of the Pope, they are nevertheless feverishly determined to carry out their programme of reform (*based on the aberrations of Teilhard de Chardin*) *in defiance of the Holy See.*"

The ring is all too clear and too close for comfort in the Archdiocese of Melbourne, Australia. Out of the welter of information in the possession of hundreds of worried parents, priests and religious, documenting attacks on almost any aspect of Catholic life during the reign of Archbishop Knox, I have selected the three main areas of worry: Catechetics (A); The Eucharistic Congress and its attack on the Doctrine of the Blessed Eucharist (B); and Priestly Training (C).

(A) The Undying Resentment against the New Catechesis

In 1970 there erupted in the pages of *The Advocate* and The *Tribune*, two Melbourne archdiocesan weeklies, a controversy about catechetics, which raged for more than six months and was finally quelled by methods that only Modernists can use in their peculiar "love" for people. But the rumblings have gone on right up to this day. It must always be borne in mind that, although we are forced to deal with catechetics seemingly separately, it was never an item in isolation. All sorts of currents were running through the Archdiocese at the time, one of the most powerful to emerge was of course the preparation to the fortieth Eucharistic Congress.

The immediate cause of the controversy was an article by the American Jesuit, Fr. Pfeifer, which appeared in *The Advocate* of 30th July 1970 in which it was stated:

> "God reveals, not so much through words as through events. Christ is met, not in doctrinal formulations, rather He is met in the experience of life."

I share the opinion of many that this statement is heretical and meant to undermine Catholic Faith, replacing it by Evolution of Dogma, Situation Ethics, Private interpretations as to the meaning of the "experiences": all fundamentally Teilhard de Chardin errors. In the article Fr. Pfeifer made it clear that this is the *"basic insight"* to the whole new way of teaching religion: the life-situation method. And right from the start of the controversy it became clear that Fr. Pfeifer's catechetics were the official catechetics of the Melbourne CCD (Confraternity for Christian Doctrine) the official body in the archdiocese dealing with religious instruction. One of the most telling observations in the controversy was made by a woman contributor who stated that, if this was such a revolutionary insight, so basic to the *whole* of catechetics, then it must surely have been brought out clearly by Vatican II. But having gone through all the Council documents, she never came across the fundamental thesis of "insight" nor any other reference remotely resembling it.

Prior to this heated debate in the Catholic press, there had appeared in the *Majellan,* a Redemptorist monthly, of January 1970 an article by Rev W Stinson, CSsR, called "Crisis in Catechetics", in which Fr. Stinson showed with remarkable insight some of the objections parents had against the catechetics, currently being canvassed as religious education. This article of Fr. Stinson brought a spate of letters to the *Majellan,* clearly showing the existence of many disturbed parents.

No serious attempts and certainly no official attempts were being made to quieten the anxiety of parents and of teachers in the early months of 1970. But at the height of the major controversy (to be precise five months after it had started in September 1970) something approaching an official attempt to do something was made. E.g. a catechetical aid called *Say Yes,* under the auspices of the Melbourne CCD, carried an article in its supplement of February 1971, entitled: "Where have all the Catechisms gone?", by Andrew Hamilton S.J,. which started as follows:

"Great changes have occurred in the Church during the last ten years or so. Many of these changes have made some of us anxious. We feel vaguely (as far as catechetics go this is certainly a misstatement: parents and teachers have been very *definite* about what they objected to) that what we have lost is good, that what we have gained to replace it has yet to prove itself. Perhaps more than anywhere else we feel this in the approaches taken to religious education in schools. At times this feeling is unspoken (oh, those modernists with their *feelings*) at other times it erupts into complaints about the strange ideas that teachers are communicating to their students: *about their mysterious reluctance to mention God or Our Lord in their classes, about the postponements of first communions, about reports that children have been told they need no longer go to Sunday Mass....*" (*My emphasis*)

The trend of the article is *not* to deny that children *do* come home with these reports nor that such drastic changes are taking place, but that these changes are for the good. A careful reading of the article will reveal more: it shows that the author, far from meeting the difficulties of the parents, exhorts them instead to an *implicit trust in the experts* and to accept the new catechetics.

This most unhappy and unfortunate trend: to ignore the parents' profound anxiety and to make out that they are to say the least *unreasonable* in being anxious, has remained the official attitude in the Archdiocese of Melbourne to this day.

But what dismayed most was the fact that this whole article, trend and all, appeared with the official imprimatur of Archbishop

Knox who had so far remained completely silent on the five months' old controversy. And so worried parents could be forgiven if they drew the conclusion "that the reluctance of the teachers to mention God or Our Lord in their classes, the postponement of First Communion attempts, and the dissolution of the obligation to attend Sunday Mass for children" carries the approval of the Archbishop of Melbourne, since the article does not deny that these things happen but tries to explain them, to make people accept them.

Supplement to *Say Yes*, Vol I, no. 3, 24th March 1971:

> "Archbishop Knox would like us to emphasise, as a matter of pastoral prudence, that we are not in any way abandoning the notion that Christ came to free us from sin in regard to the terms 'salvation-redemption'. We urge all catechists to read the article "Salvation Redemption" in *A Guide to Biblical Themes*. Cripac Press Pty Ltd, 203 Darling Rd, Caulfield East, 3145."

This little note was inserted into copies of the teacher's notes accompanying this particular issue of *Say Yes*. As a matter of pastoral prudence, extreme Teilhardism better not be taught. This printed copy is proof that at least on one occasion the teaching of *Say Yes* relative to salvation and redemption caused the Archbishop to give a corrective. If an Archbishop has reason to believe, as this one apparently had, that the modern "aids", which in reality appear as the official texts since there are *no others*, are in any way lacking in solid, sound doctrine, which don't forget the parents had been trying to tell him for the last seven months, then he has the duty to terminate it.

It is unbecoming of a bishop to try to rectify matters surreptitiously with little slips like this as inserts, and then half-apologetically ask teachers to somehow rectify matters as a matter of pastoral prudence. Note the date: for seven months now parents, teachers, catechists, nuns, brothers had been trying to tell their Archbishop that these was something seriously wrong with the catechesis of the Archdiocese. And the only positive response made so far by the Archbishop is a little note for the publishers telling them to be more prudent ...

Both *The Tribune* and *The Advocate* of 4th February 1971 report an address of His Grace, part of which was meant to reassure "parents who were agitated and worried" about the developments in the field of religious instruction in the Archdiocese of Melbourne. Here are his words:

> "Speaking of religious instruction, may I avail myself of this occasion to give some reassurances to parents who are agitated and extremely worried about developments in this field here in the Archdiocese of Melbourne. I would assure them that in the near future a magnificent document dealing with the renewal of catechetics will be available. This document was published by the Hierarchy of Italy.... Much has been written and spoken about the series known as *Come Alive*. Many of those who have written and spoken have done so without first-hand knowledge of the text.

"As Archbishop of Melbourne (at last, that sounds most official and impressive. What is he going to do?) I cherish the hope that these texts which are aids and not catechisms (where is the official catechism then?) will prove helpful to our teenagers ... etc etc."

The title of the article: "Catechetics: Archbishop Reassures Parents" (sic), made it look as if the Archbishop publicly intervened more than five months after the controversy had started, and more than a year after the alarm bells had started to ring in his own archdiocese. However, it became obvious from his speech that the Archbishop *did not meet one single specific objection or complaint* from the parents. In fact, he dismissed criticisms against one of his personally sponsored "aids", *Come Alive,* as criticisms written by many who, he claimed have no first-hand knowledge of the text; *but he failed to mention the criticisms from many who had studied the text with absolute competence and who had thoroughly rejected it.* We all know the booklet: "What is wrong with 'Come Alive'."

Furthermore, the reassurances of the Archbishop do not rest on a firm promise to put a stop to erroneous texts, nor on a firm guarantee to see to the promotion of sound doctrine as would have been his duty. He rested his assurances on two *future* documents: (1) the translation of the catechetical directory of the Italian bishops; and (2) the teacher's manual to accompany that directory. He must have been aware of the fact that 99.9% of the worried parents would *never* see these documents, let alone read them and be reassured by them. So what *does* he do then "as Archbishop of Melbourne"? He cherishes a hope ... May God have mercy on us ... Dr.

Knox appeared *deeply implicated* in the spread of spurious catechetics in his archdiocese and later on all over Australia. His whole
speech was just a sop.

The Father Maurice Duffy Affair.

In that same address Archbishop Knox announced publicly
that Fr. Maurice Duffy would prepare "an excellent teachers' manual" to go with the Directory. And so, the question is legitimate:
"Who is Father Maurice Duffy?"

Fr. Duffy answered that question himself on Monday night,
22nd March 1971, in a major address on catechetical policy in Melbourne to the combined meeting of all diocesan catechists-in-
training for 1971. (I personally attended together with many others
from Geelong.) Fr. Duffy knew that there was some explaining to
do about the way he had left the service of his own diocese of
Sandhurst (Victoria) and was almost overnight made a teacher on
catechetics at the Chadstone teacher training college, where a few
months prior to this particular meeting his very students had publicly criticized and rebuked Bishop Fox of Sale (Victoria) for ad-
dressing them at their passing-out ceremony. Apart from other
promotions in the catechetical field, Fr. Duffy was also the
"spokesman" for the Episcopal committee on catechesis.

By way of introduction that night of 22nd March, Fr. Duffy jok-
ingly and disarmingly "confessed" to his audience that he had
played the *enfant terrible* in Sandhurst, that his bishop had tried
several appointments for him, but had finally "seen the light" and
had allowed him to go to Melbourne ... laughter all round.

The first address of the evening had for sole purpose to impress on the audience that resistance to new methods of teaching is unintelligent, meaning: opposition to the life-situation method of teaching the catechism is unintelligent. The hard sell came afterwards in an address given by Fr. Duffy.

After the softening-up of the evening's first address, Fr. Duffy chose to ignore the overt references to the life-situation controversy, but it was his central theme. In a brilliant attempt he endeavoured to switch the opposition to the life-situation method into opposition to *very enlightened bishops* .... People fighting this discredited method (it was still raging in the Catholic press) suddenly found themselves fighting bishops.

The core of Fr. Duffy's address was a running commentary on the new directory of the Australian Bishops (the one referred to by Dr Knox) on the teaching of religion. Nobody had access to the text except Fr. Duffy, so that was very convenient. He really laid it on thick about the enlightened bishops. As a sign of their enlightenment he made literally the following remark:

"The very first sentence the bishops use here in this section runs like this: 'You are all teachers'. Now this is very significant. Twenty years ago the bishops would have said: 'The Pope is the Supreme teacher of the Church'. By *no longer stressing that,* the bishops want to make it clear in their enlightenment that we are all teachers."

That was the quality of his discourse. It was the only mention the Holy Father got that evening: he was mentioned incidentally as a side-issue, and even then only to get the brush-off. There was no bishop to speak in defence of the Holy Father nor to speak in defence of their own directory. A grave error of judgement was committed that night to let a man as involved in Modernism as Fr. Duffy, and who had made it clear that night that he left his own diocese under a cloud, speak for all the Bishops on such a sensitive matter as the interpretation of their own directory. But there was more to come.

As mentioned earlier: since this was an address "to the converted", catechists of the archdiocese who had been subjected to this type of catechesis for quite some time, the life-situation method hardly needed a mention; but the controversy still had to be stopped and stopped that night on the orders of the Archbishop. That this was the main issue of the evening came out when Fr. Duffy finally told his audience how Archbishop Knox had confided in him before one of his regular trips to Rome: how sorry he was to see the Catholics of Melbourne indulge in their favourite pastime tearing at each other in the press. It has to stop.

That was the clearest indication of what Fr. Duffy wanted that night. "Catholics of Melbourne stop opposing publicly the life-situation method of teaching religion. You are wounding the heart of your own archbishop."

One could not have a more complete identification of targets. Bishop Adrian was right: there are bishops who even *give orders* to allow the spread on Modernism. This was an *order* if ever there was one and Fr. Duffy made it clear from whom the order came. And this, notwithstanding the fact that *no* Catholic in Melbourne during this controversy did attack his own Archbishop. But Fr. Duffy's own students in Chadstone had publicly attacked a Bishop in the execution of his duty, not only in his presence, but also in the

Catholic press, for which no student, no Fr. Duffy, no Dr Knox has ever publicly apologized. So Fr. Duffy condones a gross and inexcusable attack on a Bishop in the Catholic press, but decries a legitimate controversy in the same press as an attack on the Archbishop himself. The inference is all too obvious: not only does Dr Knox want opposition to the life-situation method silenced, that very night Fr. Duffy pointed out to his followers how to go about achieving that: make out it is an attack on the bishops.

The immediate result of the evening is of course threefold:

(1) The Modernists are left off the hook. No longer are they required to refute the arguments of their opponents – simply hang a disloyalty charge around their necks.

(2) Because the pretence has now been created that the enlightened bishops are on the side of the life-situation innovators; the silent Church of 'old-fashioned not-with-it people and reactionaries' had been created, for whom nobody in power has cared a damn since.

(3) The Directory is now a very handy book to quote from against any bishop who dares to interfere with the life-situation innovators plans for "renewal".

The attack on Bishop Fox showed that they dared to do it with the official blessing of their Modernist teachers and that they can get away with it. On top of that the impression has now been created that the Bishops of Australia now officially teach that the Holy Father is only one of many teachers. *We* know of course better than that, but this is the type of thing that Modernists all over the place get away with nowadays (and much worse) and *they believe it.*

So that was that. The modernists closed ranks around the Archbishop against these dreadful Catholics. Fr. Duffy got another promotion: after the folding up of *The Tribune* in March 1971, at the time of this fateful night, Fr. Duffy was appointed censor of "letters to The Advocate" on catechetical matters while the most loyal editor, Cunningham, got the sack "because he did not implement the decrees of Vatican II". Both measures were taken by the Board of Directors of *The Advocate*, on which Fr. Rebeschini, private secretary to Dr Knox, has the greatest influence. Naturally with such policies and such a censor the controversy fizzled out. The silent majority were effectively muzzled. The Advocate became a truly Modernist paper. And the famous directory? Nobody in the CCD takes the slightest notice of it.

Since then there have been three petitions to the Archbishop and the Senate of Priests (one of which was even publicly discussed in The Advocate) which did not have the slightest effect. A well-known parish priest Fr D Byrne, got applauded one Sunday morning at Mass when he pointed out to his parishioners their prime duty to check the way catechetics was taught at the Catholic school. He received more than five hundred letters from all over Australia, some exceedingly revealing.

The "Parents and Friends Organization" in desperation set up its own committee to investigate the charges and was appalled at what it discovered when it checked current teaching against the *Catechetical Directory* from Cardinal Wright. Its highly documented report was just completed when Cardinal Knox left for Rome to take up his new appointment. The battle in Melbourne is far from over.

(B) The Melbourne Eucharistic Congress

The foundations of the fortieth International Eucharistic Congress were laid in Europe. It is not hard to guess by whom.

Teilhard de Chardin had no time for Eucharistic Congresses. In his 1929 essay *The Human Sense*, in which he formally broke with Catholicism (an essay so revealing and top-secret that even his atheist publishers have never dared to publish it in full for fear of giving the game away) he declares that he, Teilhard, is a privileged being who has been allowed to see that *the religious sense*, the origin, according to the Modernists of all religious experiences and religion up to now (see *Pascendi* for description and condemnation), was somehow transformed by evolution into the human sense, that is the building of the modern world.

In making this human sense the "new religion" of twentieth century man, he could not help but notice in the same essay that this clashes violently with Catholicism. And so, to give himself stature and authority *to change the Catholic Church to his own vision*, he boldly compares himself with Buddha and Muhammad, declaring that he is a figure far more serious and revolutionary and truly great then they were. He does not yet suggest in the same essay any superiority to Jesus Christ, but three years earlier, on the occasion of a Eucharistic Congress which especially enraged him when he read of it in the newspapers, he expressed the ambition *to take the spotlight away from Christ in the Eucharist*, to become the focus of the religion of the crowd of men which as yet was flocking to the Eucharist to adore it. Soon afterwards he "received the inspiration" to write *The Divine Milieu* and, as he himself expressed it, "to reveal to the general public the secret opinions about Christianity which until then he had only tried to propagate *within the seminaries.*"

To take way the spotlight from Christ in the Eucharist ... that is the clue to what happened in Melbourne, but let us start with the beginning.

1970 was a busy year for the theologians. Firstly, by then a book had appeared on the market called *Intercommunion – with Rome?*, by the Swede Dr Vilmos Vajta, director of the Centre for Ecumenical Studies at Strasbourg. Ordinary Catholics can learn a lot from this book concerning the "top people" of their own Church and about the studies in which they are engaged, with the aim of "inventing" a United World Religion. The book describes in detail how these Catholics are prepared to give up the term "transubstantiation" to replace it by the vaguer term "real presence" which Protestants could also use. They are ready to let the Sacrifice disappear, leaving nothing more than a Supper to the memorial of Christ, acceptable to all.

These "top" Catholics also want to eliminate the distinction, so clearly made by the Council of Trent, between the Catholic Priest and the Protestant Minister. The only "minor" difference would be that, while the latter is endowed from below with an ordinary charismatic ministry, the former exercise the *same ministry*, but in his case bestowed by a "sacramental rite" *carried over from a system now obsolete.*

It is of the utmost importance that the reader keeps the contents of this little book in mind for the remainder of this article. The message of the book is painfully clear: do away with the foundation laid by Christ Himself and replace it with a new one "we can all accept": a Eucharist without Transubstantiation.

Next, with these thoughts and theories clearly spelled out, the Fifth General Assembly of the Lutheran World Federation opened at Evian for a week of studies from 14th to 21st July 1970. There were some Catholic observers. The Assembly was addressed by Cardinal Willebrands. Each of the four points mentioned above were discussed and agreed upon in the modernist sense. Furthermore, the meeting condemned *Humanae Vitae* and the *Motu Proprio on Mixed Marriages* as being out of touch with present day thinking and in conflict with the views of many theologians. Dr Knutson, chairman, expressed his "concern" over the recent Encyclicals concerning the Eucharist, but also on this point he was convinced that "even problems of such delicacy as the papacy itself would lose much of their gravity if their *symbolic value* were understood".

This is exactly the same as what the radical bishops had tried to tell the Council Fathers during Vatican II. So the thought is kept alive. The Pope goes out (the foundation laid by Christ Himself) and in comes an emasculated "supper", but much more: a collegial ecumenism. The quest for power: the dream of the new ecumenism. Is it only the Protestants who talk this way?

Two months later, from 12th September to 17th September 1970, a World Congress of Theologians was held in Brussels, under the fatherly hand of Cardinal Suenens, primate of Belgium, and under the chairmanship of Professor Schillebeeckx from Holland. Taking part were Brown, Rahner, Kung, Greeley, Congar, and lesser lights, all disciples of the great names. I repeat the observation made about these men by the late Bishop Adrian:

> "These European *periti* who really imposed their theories on the bishops were themselves deeply imbued with the errors of Teilhardism and situation ethics."

Well they hadn't changed. In fact they were even more vitriolic. The theme of the Congress was "The Future of the Church", and what a future they envisage. Their clear-sightedness about the requirements of the new Teilhard de Chardin church of the future had considerably increased. In order to appreciate that, just listen to the words of Congar at the closing session:

> "The Brussels resolutions go much further than Vatican II. Because the evolution of society has accelerated since then, we can no longer content ourselves with the mere application of the conciliar texts, and *one of the difficulties facing the present pontificate is that it **does** seek to restrict itself to these.* We must ask ourselves whether the time of reforms ought not to make place now for the task of *founding the Church anew...*"

So, barely five or six years after Vatican II where the *Holy Spirit prevented* these heretics from running away with the Church, the Pope is now being accused of sticking to the decisions laid down at the Council and is being accused of not founding the Church anew by taking their advice. There is not a shadow of a doubt that these people are determined to disseminate into the Catholic camp the ideas and theories expressed by Vajta and the Lutheran Convention two months earlier, ideas which came from these people in the first place anyhow.

Hans Kung's paper was the most outspoken in undermining everything the Church had acquired from God. According to him ... "the whole message expressed in timeless and universal terms becomes just one word: Jesus Christ. All the rest is embellishment ..."

So there you have it in a nutshell: Catholic is the same as protestant because both acknowledge Jesus Christ. There is really no difference between the Catholic Mass and the Protestant communion service, or between a Priest ordained in the Catholic Church and a Protestant minister. All of this is only a matter of embellishment. Why? Because Hans Kung says so.

And just as their master Teilhard, these men are actively in the process of turning the spotlight away from Christ and turning it on themselves as the architects of this new church they are creating: the church of freedom from laws and creeds (Rahner's paper); the church of no sexual restrictions (Baum), and with a democratic government (Greely).

This is Teilhardism in practise. If these are the sentiments, thoughts, theories and determined efforts of the high priests of Teilhardism, of the men deeply imbued with his errors, then there is food for thought for any starry-eyed admirer of this "mystical poet". Because it were these very men who forced on Melbourne the hybrid Eucharistic Congress (with its Conway "Omega-Point

Play" ...), a congress that did not leave even a ripple the day after it was finished.

The first shot was fired on Tuesday, 30th September 1971, at 12.40pm, with an Australian Broadcasting Commission news item during the Victorian State news service. Here is the news item verbatim, in full, as obtained from the ABC on request:

"Leaders of nearly all major Christian denominations in Victoria have issued a joint letter calling on their congregations to work in unity to further the Christian Gospel.

The letter is signed by the heads of the Anglican, Roman Catholic, Presbyterian, Methodist, Quaker, and six other denominations.

It welcomes the strengthening of ties between Christians evident during the past year and asks church members to pray for the success of the ecumenical movement.

The letter says Christmas 1971 should be seen as a time *to reaffirm the single act of faith in Christ as being **the one essential requirement for Christian unity**.* (see **Note 1**)

Special studies to be carried out by the combined churches during the year (1972) include discussions aimed at reaching agreement *on a single form of communion service **for universal use**.* (see **Note 2**)

At today's ceremony the Roman Catholic Archbishop of Melbourne, Dr Knox, said he found it wonderful that the churches should unite in such a programme of Christian renewal. (see **Note 3**)

The Anglican Primate of Australia, Dr Woods, said he hoped 1972 would be a year in which all Christians worked together to deepen their faith and zeal." (end of ABC news item)

When the cathedral was contacted about this broadcast, Fr. Rebeschini confirmed that it was a true reflection of what had taken place. Dr Knox had given a press interview after the ceremony and most of it came from him. He divulged that a three-tier study plan was set up for next year and that other denominations would be invited to join Catholic groups in the discussions as a preparation for the Eucharistic Congress. If that is so then let us now look at **Note 1** and **Note 2.**

Note 1

If one compares these words with the one quoted above from Hans Kung's paper: the message is just one word: Jesus Christ, and if 'today's ceremony' is in preparation for the Eucharistic Congress, then it becomes obvious that 'today's ceremony' is meant to introduce *Kung's message* into the preparation for the Eucharistic Congress.

Note 2

We just saw that with his paper Hans Kung gave his blessing to the theology of Vajta's book and the Lutheran Convention. And so with these words of the broadcast the theology of Vajta and the Lutheran Convention were introduced by 'today's ceremony' into the preparation for the Eucharistic Congress. It was by now obvious that a determined attempt was being made *to turn the spotlight away from Christ in the coming congress and focus it on a Teilhard inspired ecumenism.*

If European Teilhardists had taken over the congress and its preparation, sharing Teilhard's distaste for attention given to Christ in the Blessed Eucharist and were all obsessed with his false ecumenism then it became a simple bet:

(a) That the procession would be done away with.

(b) That the Holy Father would *not* be in attendance.

(c) That it would be an ecumenical congress on Teilhard fancies of world populations, poverty, ecumenism, racism, etc. But not on Transubstantiation, the beautiful Encyclicals on the Blessed Eucharist, Mary, etc.

I still have in my possession a copy of a letter to Dr Knox in which I expressed my confidence that the Holy Father would *not* attend. The letter was dated 28th March 1972, almost a year before the Congress.

Note 3

One may think that the study of the *one communion service* was fulfilled when the thoroughly modernistic book "Unit Three: Eucharist and Life" had swept Australia, not with an imprimatur, that would have been impossible, but with Dr Knox's photo. However, as will come out later, something far more far-reaching was being carried out, something that even more riveted the European ideas to the Melbourne Archdiocese.

After the stage had been carefully set for a Teilhard-inspired congress, several things happened:

1) Many Catholics became suspicious and lost interest.

2) Many Protestants mistrusted the whole set-up and never took part.

3) The Papal Encyclical "Mystery of Faith", a jewel amongst the Papal documents, was unobtainable from the HQ, banned, forgotten, not important and was kept just as far away from the congress as the Sacred Subject-Matter would be.

4) But a complete new treatise on the Eucharist was written for the purpose, "Unit Three: Eucharist and Life", which had just as much to do with "Mystery of Faith", the Holy Father, Catholic Faith and the Blessed Eucharist as Teilhard himself.

5) The Holy Father *declined three personal invitations* to attend and instead went to a local Eucharistic Congress ...

6) The procession with the Blessed Sacrament *was* abolished. Reason given: the Anglicans requested it ...

7) A request by Dr Knox to Rome to allow the distribution of Holy Communion to *anyone* who presented him/herself at the *Statio Orbis* as a true sign of unity was turned down. After having wrecked the whole show, this would have been the final triumph of the European organizers. And so the si-

lent protest of the ecumenical service was held as a "sign of unity": *biscuits* which ought to have been Communion ...

Father Kenneth Baker, S.J. summed it all up rather well with his article in the *National Catholic Register,* entitled "Ecumenic Attempt Weakens Congress" from which the following extract:

> "*For the first time* in the history of the Congress there was no large-scale procession with the Blessed Sacrament as a public manifestation of Catholic belief in the Eucharist ... The Congress generally speaking did not attract the anticipated crowds: 100,000 visitors expected, only 20,000 turned up. Fr. Toomey expected confidently 100,000 people to turn up at the ecumenical service, the official tally was 27,000. Among the Catholics in Australia there is considerable controversy over the nature of the Congress ... A well known Australian Jesuit told me he thought the Melbourne congress would kill the whole movement started in 1881. He could be right. Catholic are not prepared to make sacrifices for a Congress *that is not really Eucharistic.*"

Whatever is touched by a Teilhard de Chardin inspired renewal looks infinitely worse after the experience than it ever looked before. The Melbourne Congress proved to be no exception. Will it be different with the Renewal of the Priesthood?

(C) The "Renewal" of the Seminary Training

The Church in Australia has had a proud record of the solid way in which she has cared for the training of her aspiring priests. There are signs in this area that another spirit has taken over, and the seminary training has become the battleground between the Spirit of God and the spirit of Teilhard. It is easy to start this topic with an *a priori*, something that goes like this. It is inconceivable that bishops who have allowed Teilhardists to dominate their CCD's would uncompromisingly and resolutely resist their dominant influence in the formation of their priests, where, according to Teilhard's own boast, he had altogether his most receptive audience years before any organized resistance was mounted against him. So it is to be expected that the seminary training in Melbourne leaves much to be desired and then leave it at that as if the case had been conclusively dealt with. I hope that people who reason like this draw the only valid conclusion and go on their knees to pray a bit more to Almighty God for their priests, and their bishops and their seminarians.

The Catholic Church has been just as clear and persistent in resisting the influence of Teilhard over the last fifty or so years as She has been clear and consistent in Her demand that the candidates for the Priesthood be solidly brought up on the philosophy of St Thomas Aquinas and the theology based on his principles. The universal disobedience to these two directives has resulted in the most ghastly confusion in priestly training. Young priests, and not so young ones too, seem to live in make-shift shelters of Bonhoefferian spirituality, Teilhardian evolutionism, Bergsonian existentialism and Protestant theology. There seems to be no end to the "renewal days" where do-it-yourself repair kits from the latest "experts" are handed out to patch up the dilapidated dwellings. In the greater Geelong area where I live, I have heard the pulpit used to declare: (1) that Adam and Eve are really only a myth, or else, they are all of us; (2) that the existence of Hell is doubtful; (3) that the Gospels are not authentic history but folklore for the use of the early Christians; (4) that Original Sin in modern theology is being accepted as being "all the evil in the world"; (5) that baptism of children means nothing, absolutely nothing, without the commitment of the parents; (6) that what remains of a man after death is the memory of him; (7) that the Church does not encourage to pray the Rosary – and this on the Feast of the Holy Rosary. I have sat through innumerable sermons on *unrelated* love, love in a vacuum ...

There appears to be utter confusion on: soul, supernatural life, (mortal) sin, grace, sanctifying grace, penance *plus* mortification, the cross and the passion, contrition, Catholic Faith, virtues, truth, and above all: the Catholic Church.

I want to make two things crystal clear here:

I do not criticize in any way a young priest: I adore what he holds in his sacred hands after the Consecration, even if he himself has a defective faith as coming out of his sermons. I am friendly with them and often like them as persons.

I completely dissociate myself, and utterly reject the explanations and aims and objectives and methods of the Australian Latin Mass Association. I am not a member, never was one, and never will be. In particular I reject their explanation that the whole confusion in the Church is caused by the *Novus Ordo*. Like anything else perfectly orthodox in the Catholic Church, the *Novus Ordo* is also subject to Teilhard de Chardin mistreatment, which can turn it into a sorry spectacle. But that is not inherent to the *Novus Ordo*.

So far we have been skirting the subject. What are the documents?

1. The official documents of the Church dealing with the formation of the candidates to the Priesthood are so numerous and detailed that it is impossible to even enumerate them here. They have not changed much over the years. The ones from Vatican II must of course be understood and interpreted in the light of what went before. They all stress holiness, interior life, union with Christ, prayer, frequent use of the Sacraments as the soundest foundation for a fruitful apostolate.

2. What about the Church's condemnations of Teilhard de Chardin.

   (a) The supreme authority of the Holy Office in a Decree dated 15th November 1957, forbade the works of de Chardin to be retained in libraries including those of Religious Institutes. His books were not to be sold in Catholic bookshops and were not to be translated into other languages.

   (b) A Decree of the Holy Office, dated 30th June 1962, under the authority of Pope John XXIII himself, warned that

"... it is obvious that in philosophical and theological matters the said works of de Chardin are replete with ambiguities or rather with serious errors that offend Catholic doctrine. That is why the Reverend Fathers of the Holy Office urge all Bishops, Superiors, Rectors to effectively protect, especially the minds of the young, against the dangers of the works of Fr. Teilhard de Chardin and *his followers*".

(c) The Vicariate of Rome in a Decree dated 30ᵗʰ September 1963, required that Catholic booksellers in Rome should withdraw from circulation the works of de Chardin together with those books which favoured his erroneous doctrines. (Pope Paul VI)

(d) The *Monita* have not been disregarded by the Holy See. A query sent to the Sacred Congregation through the Apostolic Delegate in Washington DC asking this precise question, received the following reply: "The judgements and dispositions made by the Congregation concerning the writings of Teilhard de Chardin have not been changed. Thus the *Monitum* of 30ᵗʰ June 1962 continues in effect." (8ᵗʰ March 1967)

(e) Further re-affirmations: 20ᵗʰ October 1967; 23ʳᵈ March 1970; 4ᵗʰ August 1971, coming from Apostolic Delegates on Instructions from the Congregation of the Doctrine of the Faith, remove all possible doubt on this matter.

3. In 1973 Franjo Cardinal Seper, Prefect of the Sacred Congregation for the Doctrine of the Faith had reason to write

directly to Archbishop Knox complaining about the teaching at the Archdiocesan Seminary. In his letter the Cardinal listed four objections which requested correction. They were:

(a) No Thomistic emphasis. In other words the candidates for the Priesthood were subjected to a patchwork of theological fare. There still does *not* exist a systematic philosophy course in the Melbourne Catholic College.

(b) Protestant bibliography. The significance of this will be brought out later.

(c) The dogmatic tracts on The Incarnation and on The Assumption of Mary are established Revealed Truths and many not be taught as "opinions".

(d) The *Monita* regarding Teilhard de Chardin. In other words they were not being adhered to.

If this type of intervention from Rome is necessary then it can be safely stated that a Catholic College is a breeding ground for Modernism. A Cardinal writing from Rome can obviously only write about the most obvious excesses. Non-adherence therefore to the *monita* regarding Teilhard de Chardin are considered by Cardinal Seper as a serious matter.

4. At the time of the revelation to the world of the "substantial agreement" reached between Catholic and Anglican theologians, the so-called Windsor Agreement, or Statement, Archbishop Knox revealed in *The Advocate* of 27th January

1972, that *the Presbyterian position was closer too*. Well, I have in my possession one of those very private papers used in the discussions between the Catholic and Presbyterian team. It is a paper on *Intercommunion* and is called the *Catholic* contribution. I have heard and read many statements by theologians whom I suspected to be called "heretical" by some other theologian whom I suspected to be "more in love with Plato than with truth" as the saying is. But no, the theologians will bend backwards to accommodate such a statement somehow, somewhere "within the pale". But in this case a theologian of repute who was asked to evaluate this paper had no hesitation to call the paper in part *heretical* in context. The other less damning phrases used by him were: erroneous, faulty, contrary to Church's teaching, misleading, irrelevant, grievous error ... It is for me of the utmost importance to read that this theologian calls the paper heretical where it teaches that:

> "Protestant churches have valid priesthood so that Catholics can receive Christ's Body and Blood in a Protestant communion service."

So if this is the *Catholic* contribution on an official level and the author of this paper teaches seminarians during the daytime, then Cardinal Seper's objection to Protestant bibliography takes on an ominous significance: if this is the top secret 'official' teaching in the Archdiocese of Melbourne on the Priesthood, then no seminary professor would want his students to find out from *real* Catholic books what is the *real* Catholic teaching on the Priesthood.

But there is more to it than this. I must refer the reader here once again to the Australian Broadcasting Commission's news item of 30th November 1971, as quoted previously in this article:

> "Special studies to be carried out by the combined churches during the year (1972) include discussions aimed at reaching agreement *on a single form of communion service for universal use.*"

I further remind the reader that, according to Fr. Rebeschini himself, this information was communicated to the press by Archbishop Knox himself. Now the full meaning of this news item comes home to us. Not only would the churches on a popular level discuss these matters while using the text of *Unit Three: Eucharist and Life* in preparation for the Eucharistic Congress, as requested by the European ecumenists, it now appears that the stranglehold of these theologians is even far greater: the top level discussions now reveal complete acceptance of the demands by Vajta and the Lutherans.

The ABC's broadcast not only reveals that these talks were held with the Archbishop's blessing: he was aware of the individual topics. If this "grievously erroneous" "Catholic" contribution to the discussion on Intercommunion was delivered and discussed in 1972, and the orthodox theologian's assessment was signed in February 1974, then it must have taken two years before this scandalous state of affairs was leaked out and came to light. No wonder, with this sort of "Catholic" contribution, Archbishop Knox could state in *The Advocate* of January 1972: that the Presbyterian position had come closer too.

Dr Knox's transfer to Rome is still a somewhat mysterious affair to many minds. The speculation is idle since what is available appear to be only straws in the wind. There are indications that the sudden departure from Melbourne shocked and disappointed him. In his parting words he said he was sad and sorry to leave Melbourne. Rome itself appeared to be not quite ready for him: there wasn't any time to fuse the two Secretariats he now heads, although this was the intention. So there are indications that his departure from Melbourne was hurried which point, not to a promotion, but a transfer to get him out of Melbourne.

We have seen that over the years Archbishop Knox identified himself

- with spurious catechetics and the stifling of public protests against it;
- with the probable killing of the future Eucharistic Congresses as they were known in the past in exchange for some hybrid gathering;
- with the alarming decline in the proper training of the candidates for the Priesthood;
- with the development of a false ecumenism by allowing questionable contributions in very private but top-level discussions along the lines mapped out by Vajta and the European ecumenists.

Dr Knox knew that the administration of the archdiocese was in chaos. Deep divisions appeared between him and his immediate entourage which could scarcely be kept from becoming public. The school provident fund was in great difficulties. Parishes are forced to borrow heavily against the 1975 allocation of Federal funds which are very uncertain in view of the cessation of the *per capita* rule of financing private schools. He sold Church property at less than half the market value without the consent of the Catholic Trust, as if it was *his* to dispose of. The training programme of his seminarians came under scrutiny and was in need of rebuke and correction from Rome. His disastrous catechetics course was finally rejected by his own Parents and Friends organization when it was checked against the Catechetical Directory from Rome and found gravely wanting.

Did all this require from him a final, desperate bid? Maybe we will never know, but here are the facts.

Early in May 1974, His Excellency the Apostolic Pro-Nuncio in Australia, Archbishop Gino Paro, discretely sent around to Senior Clergy, an open ballot paper, on which were to be written the names of suitable candidates as successors to Cardinal Knox.

Exactly a week later every priest of the Archdiocese of Melbourne (and goodness knows how many laypeople) received a personal letter from Cardinal Knox, asking each one, under the secrecy of the Confessional, to fill out an enclosed ballot paper with the names of the candidates of his choice, which could of course include his own (Knox's) name and to return the ballot paper directly to him in Rome. The papers had been prepared in Rome, sent in bulk to the Cathedral and from there sent to every Priest. There was an astonishing "rider" to his letter to the Priests: if for some reason people circularized *did not want to avail themselves of this opportunity to make known personally to him their choice of his successor, would they please sign the attached slip and post it to him so he could keep a record if they had received his communication ...*

These are the facts together with one more: that many Priests found this interference in ordinary canonical processes highly irregular and annoying. The imposition of the highest form of canonical secrecy, used only in the salvation of souls, to cover a scheming act, borders on intimidation and is unworthy of a Cardinal.

The Holy Father, Pope Paul VI, had stated according to the Osservatore Romano of 23rd November 1972:

> "That the watering down of the Spirit of the Gospel is a sure sign by which one can recognize the activity of the devil within the Catholic Church."

The Spirit of the Gospel is one of Eternal Truth. It is eternally opposed to the diabolical spirit of Teilhardism. Does what I have said in this article show that the Spirit of the Gospel has been at least watered down in the teachings of the Archdiocese of Melbourne during the reign of Archbishop Knox? And did we not trace this "watering down" to the diabolical spirit of Teilhardism to which most of the Catholic life in the Archdiocese became gradually subjected? And is it too much to speak of a *hidden schism*?

Chapter Four

The Fatal Consequences of this Worldwide Schism

Hidden schisms have a habit of breaking out into the open. Our description of the aftermath of Vatican II within the boundaries of the Melbourne Archdiocese will be recognized by many as being the true picture of things the world over. You do not have to be a regular reader of the many excellent publications and periodicals which keep the Light of Faith burning, to realize that literally thousands of Catholics have been trying for years now to tell their bishops that there is something seriously wrong, not only with the interpretations and implementations of the Decrees and Spirit of Vatican II but also with the general paralysis and silence of Hierarchies in the face of it. Some, mainly the members of the Latin Mass Associations, at least in Australia, have gone over-board in declaring Vatican II itself heretical and evil and consequently also His Holiness Pope Paul VI. They are obviously floundering in a make-belief of their own. But there are millions of good, solid staunch Catholics the world over who love the Holy Father and their Bishops and Priests, who love the Church as they have known it and still recognize it, who, because they have kept their Supernatural Catholic Faith and the Light it contains, trust the Holy Spirit in their innate abhorrence of anything that is tainted with the diabolical spirit of Modernism, *and who are still mistrusted by their bishops.*

The Bishops, apparently seem to be of the opinion, when they close their doors and their hearts and their Catholic weeklies and their eyes and their ears to these Catholics, that they should trust the Holy Spirit more in the type of renewal, that they, the bishops, propose. I think personally that it should be the other way round: the bishops should trust the Holy Spirit more as motivating these Catholic not to accept just any renewal as coming from Vatican II.

I think that quite a number of responsible people within the Catholic Church have come to the conclusion that there is developing today, what Cardinal Newman so aptly described as a "suspense in the function of the teaching Church" during the sixty-year period of the Arian heresy. Although Cardinal Newman was called to Rome over his statement, he was nevertheless vindicated, and his pending canonization proves his works are free from error. For a detailed discussion of this very interesting topic read: *Cardinal Newman and Authority in the Church*, by the Rt. Rev. Mgr. Philip Flanagan, D.D., Ph. D., issued as an *Approaches* supplement.

From what we can gather this Hidden Schism is worldwide. A large section of Christendom has (for reasons we were at pains to explain in this article) *voluntarily* placed itself in a modernist camp guided by the principles of Teilhard. The natural outcome for a large section of Christendom, which voluntarily selected to be guided by Teilhard de Chardin interpretations of Vatican II, is to be *ruled* for a while by a head of their own making. To be *ruled* by an anti-pope, the greatest evil that can befall a considerable section of Christendom (for the true Church, however small, will *never* be ruled by an anti-pope even if leaderless for a time) must be seen as a severe punishment by God for the greatest crime of all: corporate apostasy.

And so, people who liked to listen to Teilhard and his interpretations of Catholicism in order to be encouraged to follow their own consciences, are people with "itching ears, always eager to hear something fresh" as St Paul warned us would happen in 2 Tim 4. 4., by a "pope" who will make it all "official".

I fully realize of course that we are entering very dangerous ground here, but as always, I am guided by documentation. Before, however, acquainting you with the evidence we have, I want to make a couple of points clear.

1. It is quite within the bounds of the possible that the schismatic Teilhard-church can foist on the world by unlawful means an anti-pope, preventing for a while the selection of a true pope, and that this anti-pope will falsely unite Christendom in a United World Religion: the dream of communists, freemasons, and modernists. Since this aspect so obviously touches on what I have called a parallel development in secular society, it is of the utmost importance that one branch out sideways and *study* this parallel development.

2. If, out of the turmoil and ferment sweeping the Church at present time, a successor to the See of Peter is one day chosen, and he looks to us a most unsuitable candidate, we cannot, on that fact alone, reject him. For, if he is a lawfully chosen pope, he will be protected from heresy preaching like all his predecessors under the normal conditions for in-

fallibility. And on the other hand, if an ostensibly neutral anti-pope is foisted on the Church by unlawful means, then he will obviously *not* be protected by this tremendous privilege, no matter how the schismatics will force on the Church his decisions as binding. In other words, we *cannot* go by the colour of the man in the tiara, nor by the mode of his selection, which will be secret.

Here we can only do what St. Thomas taught us in his beautiful hymn *Adoro Te Devote*: "Sed auditu solo tuto creditor". "We can only safely believe when *hearing*". When the man with the tiara opens his mouth to contradict another Pope's teaching, then we safely know. So, here again, it is stressed that we must know our Catholic Faith. As we all know so well: *listening to the Holy Father* is not a pastime specifically encouraged by the Teilhardians, but it will be forced upon us if and when they get their man usurping the throne of St. Peter.

For the evidence of all this I will stick to specifically Catholic documentation, but as said before, there is in contemporary secular literature overwhelming evidence that we are approaching a climax of sorts that cannot be ignored.

To facilitate this process of making an anti-pope appear to be the real thing, the Modernists, in anticipation and with careful preparation, have forced upon the Church a whole host of their pet ideas, so that all their man will eventually have to do is *to confirm what had already previously been "taught"*. It is precisely in this area that the silence of most bishops has created the same "suspense in the function of the teaching Church" (with the exception of the

Holy Father and some very courageous bishops) as confused the Church for sixty years under Arianism in the fourth century. For, if Teilhard de Chardin errors did appear with imprimaturs in all sorts of publications, from CCD handouts and "aids" to Unit Three, Our Living Faith, Dutch Catechism, etc, and they were not opposed by the majority of bishops, then an anti-pope will have no trouble "proving" that it was taught before and all he does is to confirm the fact.

There have been made several attempts, at least three that I know of by *The Advocate*, the one-time weekly of the Melbourne Archdiocese, to directly link the Holy Father with spurious teachings. And where they could not directly implicate the Holy Father, the Modernists – as we all know only too well – have made innumerable attempts to make out that their teaching is the official teaching of the Church. Let us analyse some of their more glaring attempts, starting with the three incidents in *The Advocate*.

1. In the issue of 6th July 1972, there appeared a review of a book on Original Sin. The book was written by Fr. Henri Rondet, the review by Fr. J. P. Kenny, S.J. Apart from the fact that the erroneous tenets of both the book and the review run counter to Trent, (Denz, 1511), Holy Scripture (Romans 5. 12) and Tradition echoed by Pope Paul, the erroneous implication made here for all readers to accept is that a *personal* sin of Adam is *not* revealed truth, is *not* defined truth, can be relegated to oblivion and is still subject to dispute and argument. The tone of the review is such

that the official teaching of the Church is held up for contempt and ridicule. Here is a quote from it:

> "Rondet is a positive scholar, certainly not a creative thinker of the calibre of Rahner, Teilhard de Chardin, or Congar. Something much bolder than Rondet's rather timorous and backward looking attempt is needed if a theologian is going to *reformulate* the Dogma of Original Sin (where did we hear that phrase before?) along the lines mapped out by Vatican II or Pope Paul." (And then follows a speech by Pope Paul which, as can be expected, has nothing whatsoever to do with the reformulation of the Dogma of Original Sin.)

To quote the Holy Father here as being on the side of the heresies of Teilhard is a gratuitous insult and should not have been allowed to happen by The Advocate or Dr. Knox. So, to settle the argument, let us quote what the Holy Father *did say* about Original Sin in his famous (but never quoted) *Credo of the People of God* (which of course should have been done by Archbishop Knox as soon as this rubbish appeared in his newspaper):

> "The Fall. We believe that in Adam all have sinned, which means that the original offence committed *by him* caused human nature, common to all, to fall to a state in which it bears the consequences of that offence and which is not the state in which it was first in our *first parents*, established as they were in holiness and justice and in which man knew neither evil nor

death. It is human nature so fallen, stripped of the grace that clothed it, injured in its own natural powers and subjected to the dominion of death, that is transmitted to all men and it is in this sense that every man is born in sin."

All this is utterly rejected by Teilhard and anyone, like Fr. Kenny, who advocates polygenism. We must not forget that it was this same Fr. Kenny who wrote the paper on intercommunion, who teaches the candidates for the Priesthood in the Catholic College at Clayton his erroneous ideas on the Catholic Priesthood, and he is also the one who teaches the tracts on the Incarnation and Mary's Assumption, of which Cardinal Seper wrote they are established truths. He has the above reviewed book of Rondet on his booklist for his students. Why reveal this man's identity? Because only a few days ago I served the Mass of one of his "products": a young priest straight from seminary, awaiting his first appointment. This young man had obliterated from his Mass not only every reference to sin but the actual word "sin".

Let us call to mind our sins, became a complete fabrication of his own. In your mercy keep us free from *sin*, became free from selfishness. Look not on our *sins* but on the faith of your Church, became again: look not on our selfishness. But the worst example of his absolute disbelief in sin came when he had to show the Host and say: this is the Lamb of God who takes away the sins of the world. This he changed into his own fabrication: this is Jesus Christ who gives us his spirit. Happy are they, etc.

This is what happens when Teilhard de Chardin followers are allowed free rein not only to introduce the ideas of Vajta, the Lutheran Assembly, the World Congress of Theologians into the Catholic Church, *but to teach it and to make out that it is the official teaching of the Church*. In order that a poor unsuspecting seminarian *loses his faith in the sacrifice of the Mass*, he must first lose his belief in *Sin*, which will follow *naturally from the rejection of the Dogma of Original Sin*, called by Teilhard nothing more startling than a mistake in selecting the right expression, at their stage of development in evolution, of a certain group of people.

In this Mass the hidden schism came out into the open. Pope Paul VI has absolutely forbidden any changes in the format of the New Missal. These people take *no notice*. Cardinal Seper could have saved his breath and his paper. And if bishops do not take notice and do not take action, a future anti-pope will have no difficulty in showing that this type of teaching was allowed to flourish under a previous pope.

So there is the first example, the classic example, of how the Modernist works under the very nose of the Hierarchy: make out that the Holy Father or the Church is already on their side and boldly claim approval. If nobody objects ...

2. Now that we have seen the method in action, let us take a look at another example. In The Advocate of 27th January 1972, there appeared an article under the heading: "Priest's Red China Views Dismay Taiwan Clergy". In it we read that Fr. Wei, 68, has called for the recognition of the position of bishops unlawfully consecrated in Communist China. "While in Rome, Fr. Wei said that five years ago *Pope Paul had privately expressed strong reservations about the*

indiscriminate recognition of illegally consecrated bishops without the examination of individual cases."

This is spurious, mischievous reporting and should have been verified. Fr. Wei makes out as if Pope Paul's "reservation" is one of degree and could be bought if the price was right. Spreading this sort of report about Pope Paul and see it cause no ripple, will make it very easy for an anti-pope later on to recognize apostate bishops and unholy "Masses". I am convinced that Pope Paul won't have a bar of indiscriminate recognition. Only Communists would like to see their puppets recognized indiscriminately and on a scale to force their will on Catholics.

3.   A very important notion nowadays is Pluralism. The Modernists would love to see the principle of *pluralism in doctrine* adopted. It would make every "Christian" a Catholic and we would have unity. The Holy Father is very definite about the use of the word. But, again, he appears to be the only one, at least in public pronouncements.

In *The Advocate* of 7th October 1971, we read in the article *Fears Subside at Catechetics Talks* the following statement:

"The exchange of ideas and experiences made it clear that *both Rome* and the National Hierarchies regard pluralism not as a temporary phenomenon to be overcome, *but as the very foundation of Catholicism.*"

Is *Rome* here the Holy Father? Does Pope Paul really believe this meaning of pluralism? Why did he not say so when he spoke about it? The appearance has again been created that the Holy Father is on the side of modern ideas and with a little push can be made to appear to teach that pluralism lies at the foundation of Catholicism and *ipso facto* of Catholic Faith because it is Catholic Faith that lies at the foundation of Catholicism. Consequently the sentence in the above quote is very misleading because the Pope rejects any use of the word "pluralism" as being at the foundation of Catholic Faith. This is what he said when he spoke about pluralism in Sydney, Dec 1970.

> "One may ask: Is pluralism admitted? Yes, but the significance of this word must be well understood. It must on *no account contradict* the substantial unity of Christianity. Some of the dangers that lie hidden in pluralism occur when it is not limited to the *contingent forms of religious life*, but presumes to authorize individual and arbitrary interpretations of Catholic Dogma, or when it prescinds in *theological study* from authentic Tradition."

"Contingent forms of religious life" is something very different from "the very foundations of Catholicism". If all we had was the quote from *The Advocate* to go by, how would we be able to distinguish a possible anti-pope if he also taught as "Rome and the National Hierarchies" already do, that pluralism does lie at the foundation of Catholicism and *ipso facto* at the foundations of Catholic

Faith? He would then contradict Pope Paul's teaching, but what if nobody quotes Pope Paul's teaching?

And so the struggle for the mind of the Pope, the mind of the Church goes on; unceasingly, unrelentingly, day and night: the Modernists, with all the powerful means of propaganda at their disposal, claiming to have the mind of the Pope and the mind of the Church on their side – preparing for the day when a pope of their own making will approve of the church of their own making, teaching the doctrines of their own making.

In conclusion it would now suffice to just list a few pet doctrines of the Modernists, which they would love to see adopted by the Universal Church. None of the following have ever been touched by a Successor of Peter, so if a future one does, watch out and listen very attentively.

> ➤ They want to see the "substantial agreement" between Anglican and Roman Catholic theologians on the blessed Eucharist and holy orders ratified.
> ➤ They want to see this extended to all other communion services by means of the One Communion Service For Universal Use, with recognition of each other's ministers to "effect the Eucharist".
> ➤ In this respect they want the words of the Consecration "updated" so that a Eucharist without Transubstantiation will become the new centre of unity acceptable to all, a simple memorial service.

➢ They want the Papacy *effectively* limited through collegiality as the new principle of decision making.

➢ They want the Decrees against Teilhard de Chardin and his teaching revoked.

➢ In order to have their longed-for Council of Reconciliation in Jerusalem where all Christians can participate in true ecumenical fashion and whose decrees will then be binding on all, they will then teach that they have effected the reunion of all Christendom *based on love*, against the 1928 encyclical *Mortalium Animos* of Pope Pius XI.

➢ On the side of Morals they want a cautious introduction of birth control, optional celibacy and a lot of other freedoms based on individual consciences.

➢ They want the principle of Pluralism in Doctrine accepted.

Since Modernism is essentially a religion of reason and no longer of believing in revealed, defined Truths, and since all the points mentioned above (and many more) sound so "reasonable" many who have lost their Catholic Faith, or who have *lost the love* for their Catholic Faith and so a knowledge of it, and who no longer care "one way or the other", such people will no longer be in a position to distinguish a true Successor of Peter from a possible *false* one. And so they will drift along. In a vague sort of way they have "heard it all before", somewhere, sometime, and so it is probably good ...

"To the rest of you I say: do what the Elders tell you and wrap yourselves in humility to be servants of each other, because God refuses the proud and will always favour the humble. Bow down then before the power of God now and He will raise you up on the appointed day; unload all your worries on Him since He is looking after you. **Be calm but vigilant**, because your enemy the devil is prowling around like a roaring lion looking for something to eat. **Stand up to him**, strong in Faith and in the knowledge **that your brothers all over the world are suffering the same things**. You will have to suffer only for a little while: the God of all grace who called you to eternal glory in Christ will see that all is well again. He will confirm, strengthen and support you. His power lasts for ever and ever. Amen." (1 Peter 5. 5 – 11.)

Book III

The 'Theology' of
the Late Pierre Teilhard de Chardin S.J.

Frits Albers, Ph.B.,
(1st Edition 1979, Revision 1997)

Section I

Quotes from Teilhard's work together with extensive Comments which allow readers to come to grips with the essential elements of what has become known as 'his theology'.

Our Blessed Lord has said that, towards the end, there would come a period in which - if it were possible - even the Elect would be deceived, and that, because of His Elect, those days would be shortened. Since the late thirties and early forties, when disobedient Jesuit Professors began introducing the principles of Pierre Teilhard de Chardin's philosophical and theological assertions in their houses of study in Nijmegen (Holland) and Louvain (Belgium), replacing pure Thomism, there has been no end to their efforts to introduce the thoughts of Teilhard into every Institute of Higher Learning within the Catholic Church. This is deception. (See for details of their concerted efforts my 1974 work *Teilhard de Chardin and the Dutch Catechism*). The latest element added to this deception is now to discard the 'syringe' Teilhard now that his poison has been firmly injected into the courses of study in what used to be called 'the Seminaries'. It is becoming increasingly more fashionable to refer to Teilhard as a brilliant scientist but to call him a poor theologian. This is only intended to darken even more the original deception by excluding more and more light. It is perfectly true to say that Teilhard de Chardin was neither a scientist nor a theologian. But what the disclaimer 'poor theologian' means to convey is, that Teilhard had no influence at all on theology. And that is the lie of the century. It is a safe bet that it was not as a scientist that the 'mystical poet Teilhard' influenced and corrupted Catholic thinking to the four corners of the globe. His lasting influence lies in a totally different sphere.

Quote 1[1]

"What increasingly dominates my interest is the effort to establish within myself and to diffuse around me A NEW RELIGION whose personal god is the soul of the world, as demanded by the cultural and religious stage we have reached."

We will be able to prove that these words of Teilhard de Chardin contain the clue to the fundamental cause for the unprecedented upheaval in modern Catholic thinking. We will find ample reason to conclude that any 'theology' based on these premises is not a theology at all, but in fact nothing more than a faulty course in comparative cultural humanism and Marxism.

Teilhard de Chardin himself gave us the clearest explanation of what he meant by 'a new religion':

Quote 2[2]

"I have come to the conclusion that, in order to pay for a drastic valorisation and amortisation of the substance of things, a whole series of reshaping of certain representations or attitudes, which seem to us definitely fixed by Catholic Dogma, has become necessary if we sincerely wish to Christify evolution. Seen thus, and

---

[1] *Letters to Leontine Zantha*. Collins, 1969. Jan 26, 1936, p. 114.
[2] Teilhard de Chardin, *Stuff of The Universe*, 1953.

because of an ineluctable necessity, one could say that a hitherto
UNKNOWN FORM OF RELIGION is gradually germinating in
the heart of modern man, in the furrow opened by the idea of evolution."

This goes to the heart of the modern problem. Catholicism
cannot, not even with the wildest stretch of the imagination, be
truthfully called "a hitherto unknown form of religion". So Teilhard admits that it is no longer Catholicism which he sees gradually germinating in the heart of modern man. Yet it is Catholic
Dogma which is to be bent and twisted and reshaped and reformu-
lated in order to make this 'new religion' appear to be Catholic. No
one but Teilhard himself could put it as clear as this! No one but
Teilhard himself must be heard first on what Teilhardism is all
about! At least the man himself does not leave us in any doubt, in
spite of the number of cloaks his innumerable followers may have
found it necessary to put discreetly over the soulless corpse of his
lifeless Catholicity!

Quote 3[3]

"I consider that the reformation in question (much more profound than the one of the 16th century) is no longer a simple matter of institutions and ethics, BUT OF FAITH. In the course of the

---

[3] "Letter to ex-Dominican G.", Oct 4, 1950. *Approaches*, 1966, printed
this letter in full in its original French and the English translation. The
letter is also quoted in *The Truth About Teilhard de Chardin* by Mgr. Leo
S. Schumacher, and in *Le Concile et Teilhard*, Maxime Gorce, 1963, p.
197.

last 50 years I have watched the revitalization of Catholic thought and life taking place around me in spite of the encyclicals - too closely not to have unbounded confidence in the ability of the old Roman stem to revivify itself. Let us then each work in our separate spheres: all upward movements converge."

Quote 4[4]

"Let us then acknowledge the situation honestly: Not only *The Imitation of Christ*, but also the Gospel itself needs to undergo this correction, and the whole world will make them undergo it!"

"...but of Faith". A reformation of Faith (his words), a correction of Faith and of the Gospels (his words), more thorough than the Reformation of the 16th century. Yes indeed, here we are staring at the dead remains of Teilhard's Catholicity, hailed by all the modernists as the new 'life-in-the-spirit' and as the fundamental outlook of the 'new theology'. A correction of Catholic Faith demanded by Teilhard as the great and universal correction the whole world will force on the Church. Forced on the Church by the world? By that one thing the Founder of the Church came to redeem us from, and for which He refused to pray at the Last Supper? Because (as St. John explains) the world, the total antithesis of the Incarnation, is totally alien to the Master's Gospel. This is dramatically restated by Teilhard when he observes that the 'correction enforced upon the Church by the whole world' is "in spite of the encyclicals"! A revitalization in spite of the encyclicals is not a

---

[4] *The Human Sense*, 1929. See remarks in the next quoted Source, No. 5.

revitalization at all but a reversal to heresy and its ensuing barbarism. And it has been clearly spelled out here by the only author who is best qualified to speak on the wording and the meaning of his own writings, that the "furrow" to which "this hitherto unknown form of religion", this new seed of heresy and barbarism, is being entrusted and in which it will germinate, is the furrow opened by the idea of evolution.

This fulfils most accurately what Pope St. Pius X observed and predicted would happen in two separate documents. In one of them, being one of those encyclicals dismissed by Teilhard, the holy Pope wrote:

"They lay the axe not to the branches and shoots, but to the very root, i.e. to the Faith and its deepest fibres. And once having struck at this Root of Immortality, they proceed to diffuse poison through the whole tree." (*Pascendi*, 1907)

Teilhard insists that it is a matter of Faith. And so in another document, the great Saint Pius X, after having condemned a popular movement in France which went by the name of the *Sillon* (which significantly is French for 'Furrow'!), for "having become no more than a miserable affluent (tributary) to the great movement of apostasy being organised in every country for the establishment of the 'One-World Church'", and after having assured us in no uncertain terms that "we know only too well the dark workshops in which are elaborated these mischievous doctrines which ought not to seduce clear-thinking minds," drives home the monumental truth of how people become part of a miserable stream feeding the great movement of apostasy, and how, after all that bending and twisting and reshaping and reformulating of what appears fixed by Catholic Dogma, they end up in the One-World Church of Darkness when he wrote those immortal words:

"They have been carried away to another gospel which they thought was the true Gospel of Our Saviour." (*Our Apostolic Mandate*, 1910)

So here it is. Teilhard wants us to look at the situation "honestly". We must acknowledge with him (1) that modern man wants his "correction"; (2) that it can only be brought about by "twisting and bending what appears fixed by Catholic Dogma"; (3) that it must be presented as "Catholic"; (4) that it involves a "new faith"; and (5) that "the whole world" will enforce all this on the Church! So too do we have here its condemnation.

This is absolutely what Teilhard de Chardin wanted and what his innumerable Modernist followers still want: they crave for 'another gospel'. They want a "hitherto unknown form of religion" made to appear as the Catholic Religion i.e. 'as the true Gospel of Jesus Christ', through the twisting and bending and refashioning "of what seems to us fixed by Catholic Dogma".

And that is precisely what this present study will be all about.

As was to be expected, Teilhard also provides us with a splendid example of what he himself understood by this "reshaping of what appears definitely fixed by Catholic Dogma":

Quote 5[5]

"Without exaggeration one can say 'Original Sin', in the formulation still current today, is one of the principal obstacles to the intensive and extensive movement of progress in Christian thought. An embarrassment or scandal (it is Catholic Dogma he is talking about here!) for those of goodwill at the same time that it is a refuge for narrow spirits". (Teilhard's definition of obedience to Catholic Faith!).

"Let us then pose as a point of departure (departure from Dogma, no doubt: here begins his 'twisting and bending and re-

---

[5] This long quote is from Teilhard's third attack on the Catholic Dogma of Original Sin. His first attack was contained in an untitled, unpublished paper in 1922, the one that landed by mistake in Rome, causing an uproar. His second attack is contained in his 1929 essay *The Human Sense* containing his formal break with the Catholic Church. His third attack was delivered in another untitled, unpublished paper of 1947. Eventually the 1st and 3rd paper were published in *Christianity and Evolution*, Collins, 1971, under the respective titles "Notes on some possible historical representations of Original Sin" (1922), and "Reflections on Original Sin" (1947). The middle paper, *The Human Sense* of 1929, appeared eventually in a diluted form in *Towards the Future*, Collins, 1975. All of these works are in my possession, but my quotations are taken from a much earlier translation from the original French of these three papers, which appeared in two consecutive issues of *Triumph*, an orthodox American monthly magazine, Nov and Dec 1971, which provide us with the undiluted, and so much stronger, language in which the teilhardian attack on Original Sin and related Catholic teachings appears. These *Triumph* articles too are in my library in their original, i.e. non-photocopied, form.

shaping and reformulating') that since the Multiple, that is non-being in a pure state, is the sole rational form of a creatable non-being, or 'creable', the creative act is only intelligible as a gradual process of arrangement and unification. This fact (FACT!!) leads one to admit that 'to create is to unify'".

"In such a universe in which the Multiple is the primordial non-sinful creatable form of Nothingness, the functional equivalent of the first Adam, source of statistical evil, the intellectual problem of evil disappears. Since in this perspective, in effect, physical suffering and moral faults are introduced INEVITABLY (his stress) into the world under the heading of a by-product of statistically inevitable (his stress) of the unification of the Multiple.

"In this explanation (sic!) Original Sin undoubtedly ceases to be an isolated act ...."

As every Catholic by now has come to expect: this prototype of twisting and bending and reshaping results in a total denial of the original Dogma. And of course, it did not stop there. We have the above-quoted words of the same Pope and Saint for that:

"And once having struck at this root of immortality, they proceed to diffuse poison through the whole tree, so that there is no part of Catholic Truth which they leave untouched, none that they do not strive to corrupt." (*Pascendi*, 1907)

Since it is obvious that such a twisted wreck can never be graced with the glorious name of Catholic Theology, which is only reserved for one thing, and (because of merciless historical criticism) cannot even hope to be posthumously epitaphed: 'Here lies Catholic theology gone wrong', we have to examine the bits and pieces scattered over Teilhard's writings, to come across the booby-trap which made this whole 'theology' self-destructive in X years and blew out the brains of all those who espoused it. ("Cologne Declaration", e.g.)

One track that leads into the tangled web of Teilhard's torturous mental activity is his preposterous claim, that no proper system of thought existed prior to his evolutionary insights. I must warn the reader that what is going to be opened up here, is nothing less than the tragedy of a corporate mental breakdown, and that we are entering a desolate, windswept area, scene of Twentieth Century foremost mass intellectual suicide pact amongst Catholic intelligentsia. NOTHING will make sense! But this tragic conviction of the uniqueness of his own insights prevails in Teilhard's *Le Milieu Divin* (1926), in *The Phenomenon of Man* (1930) and flowed from these into all his other works as their foundation and *raison d'etre*. In his 1929 article *The Human Sense* in which he formally broke with the Catholic Church, an article so revealing and top-secret, that not even his atheist publishers dared to print it in full for fear of giving the game away, he declares of himself that he, Teilhard, is a privileged being who has been allowed to see that the 'religious sense' (See Note 1) was somehow transformed into 'the human sense' by evolution, forcing him to turn his back on building 'the kingdom of God' in preference to 'Building the Earth' (the title of one of his books).

(Note 1. According to the Modernists, the 'religious sense' is not Supernatural, but is on the natural level the origin of all religious experience. In *Pascendi* Pope St. Pius X gives a description and a thorough condemnation of this utter fallacy.)

In making this 'human sense' and this 'building of the modern world' into the 'religion' of modern man in the Twentieth Century, he could not help but notice in the same article that all this clashes violently with Catholicism. And so to give himself stature and authority 'to change the Catholic Church to his own vision', he boldly compares himself with Budda and Mohammed, declaring that he is a figure far more serious and revolutionary and truly great than they were.

So then, what is his 'thesis'? What is his 'starting point'? What is that 'fundamental insight' so all-embracing and unique that, whoever shared it with him, or even applauded him for having it, perished with him on that lonely mental outpost, far removed from the saving constraints of the Truths of Catholic Faith? I will print it here in full from *The Phenomenon of Man*:

Quote 6[6]

"Blind indeed are those who do not see the sweep of a movement whose orbit *infinitely transcends* the natural sciences (See Note 2) and has successfully invaded and conquered the surrounding territory: chemistry, physics, sociology, and even mathematics and the history of religions. One after the other all the fields of human knowledge (theology!) have been shaken and carried away by the same underwater current in the direction of the study of some development. Is evolution a theory, a system or a hypothesis? It is much more: it is the general condition to which all theories, all

---

[6] *The Phenomenon of Man*. Fontana (Collins), 1965, p. 241.

hypotheses, all systems must bow and which they must satisfy henceforward if they are to be thinkable and true. Evolution is a curve that all lines must follow".

(Note 2. Only the Divine Being, God, can infinitely transcend natural sciences and all the rest of creation. Teilhard asserts here that evolution does that. He is changing the concepts of God and Creation, hoping that, by changing the concepts themselves, the contents of these concepts, the Realities they hold, will also change.)

Then Teilhard continues to show that only now there has emerged:

Quote 7[7]

"the birth of an entirely new universe"

... through modern man's awareness of evolution. Until that time according to him, the world seemed to rest, static and frag-mentable, on the three axes of its geometry. (I always thought that it was firmly sustained by God's Power and Providence, and by the Redemption won by Christ His Son). Then Teilhard expresses clearly for us not only our unspoken question but also his answer:

"What makes and classifies a 'modern man'?"

---

[7] Ibid. p.241.

Quote 8[8]

"Having become capable of seeing in terms, not of space and time only, but also of biological space-time; and <u>above all</u> (my stress): of having become incapable of seeing anything otherwise, anything, <u>not even himself</u>". (Teilhard's stress)".

Having thoroughly grasped what is being said here, all we have to do is follow the thread right through Teilhard's impossible 'philosophy', right through modern 'theology', modern catechesis and morality, through Kohlberg, Marxism, Freemasonry straight into the bowels of the One-World 'Church of Darkness'.

The implications of what is being said here are colossal.

Four things stand out: two assertions and two immediate conclusions.

Assertion No. 1.

BIOLOGICAL space-time is the only supreme, existing reality. It is evolution and evolution is it! They are synonymous. It is all there is, all 'reality'. Everything must satisfy this "in order to be thinkable and true".

Assertion No. 2.

Modern man, the modern Christian, the modern Catholic is only true and thinkable if he has become incapable of seeing anything differently, anything more than this.

---

[8] Ibid. pp.241-242.

Conclusion No. 1.

Outside biological space-time: evolution, there is nothing else. No separate God, no supernatural realities. Biological space-time is the home for the evolving god living in its 'Divine Milieu'. Outside that 'god' no other God can be postulated. The evolving god is part, the soul, of evolution. He too can only be "thinkable and true" if understood as part of evolution.

Conclusion No. 2.

By inserting here the word 'biological', Teilhard has given us the origin of the 'cosmic-Christ'. The 'cosmic-Christ' is extended by biology, which in Teilhardian language and in all modern 'understanding' ('married priests' included) means: sexual propagation. Remember there is no other Christ as we "have become incapable of seeing anything else, including ourselves". WE are the 'cosmic-Christ'.

What all this does of course is lay the foundation for the rampant impurity of our days. This is how it is taught. This is the foundation of encouraging masturbation, free love, premarital sex, the pill: any sex propagates the biological 'Christ', the 'cosmic-Christ'.

In biological space-time there is no longer sin, no longer need for confession, no longer the need to fear the loss of the Supernatural: it doesn't exist! No matter what we do (the essence of the totally ineffectual 'existential act') evolution will make sure that we end up inevitably in 'god-omega', the endpoint of evolution: In evolution there is no longer any need nor any room for a separate Catholic Church: evolution takes care of everything since its final end in 'god-omega' is assured, inevitable. 'God' evolves with evolution as its 'soul'.

No wonder Pope St. Pius X gave to this total break-down of any doctrine the name "miserable affluent, feeding the great movement of apostasy organised in every country". But the unprecedented paralysis of the world's episcopal body in the face of this 'theology', this 'catechesis', no matter how careful the language is in which all this 'teaching' has been couched, has shown that bishops are unsure if this is nowadays true Catholic teaching or not; are unsure if this must be vigorously resisted or not. It is not asserted here that bishops are (yet) teaching this: it is asserted here that the silence and timidity of the bishops in the face of the unmistakable Teilhardian contents in modern 'theology' and 'catechesis' clearly show that bishops can no longer tell the difference. And they are paying dearly for this studious insult of the Catholic Church.

Teilhard is quite specific here, and all his future work ("the eternal feminine", "the evolution of chastity', etc) show him also to be quite unrepentant. If in the course of centuries through, what he considers "a static cosmology", the wrong idea of a Personal God has developed, even backed by Revelation, a creating God so independent of His creation and creatures that they add nothing to His glory, His being and His perfection, so that all creation must bow to Him in order to be thinkable and true, then Teilhard will now declare that this is not so. That even God is bound by evolution, must follow its "infinitely transcending sweep", and must obey the "laws of evolution" in order to be thinkable and true Himself. He must be part of evolution, but a privileged part: its 'soul'.

The immediate other consequences of all this nonsense are:

1. Teilhard is greater than God because Teilhard allocates to God His place, His role and His function in evolution.
2. Teilhard denies God the omnipotence of creating from nothing *creatio ex nihilo*. He is quite adamant in this. God has been part of this evolutionary process, this 'divine milieu' since its inception. According to Teilhard, whatever he calls "the God of evolution" can only rearrange and unite pre-existing material. (See Quote 3 above)
3. Teilhard denies God the power to perform miracles.

In two 1920 articles in which Teilhard initiated 'research' into the impossibility of *creatio ex nihilo*, into the impossibility of the existence of Adam and Eve, into the impossibility of the Fall (and so into the impossibility of the Redemption by Christ), he also started to develop his ideas about the impossibility of miracles:

Quote 9[9]

"This property of the divine of being inapprehensible to any material grasp has always been emphasised in connection with the miraculous. Except for the cases of the restoration of life to the dead (which are extremely rare and, apart from those recorded in

---

[9] *Christianity and Evolution.* Collins, 1971. "Notes on the modes of divine action in the universe", 1920, p. 28-29.

the Gospel, all more or less arguable) there are in the history of the Church no miracles that cannot be explained by vital forces that have been remarkably augmented in their own direction (Teilhard's stress). We may be quite certain then that, the more miracles are studied, the more they will be found to be extensions of biology."

Again that pre-eminence allotted to biology (evolution) over divine power.

Most of us are aware that the whole catechesis built on this sort of 'theology' makes of the Gospels no more than folklore, denying them any authenticity and historical objectivity (to say nothing of inerrant Divine Inspiration!), so that Teilhardian Modernists can painlessly do away with even the rare cases of restoration to life recorded in Sacred Scripture. And in case we did not hear him too well, Teilhard then goes on:

Quote 10[10]

"In so far we can judge the progress of the world, God's power has not so free a field of action as we assume: on the contrary, in virtue of the very constitution of the 'participated being' (i.e. creatures which must help God create as explained (!) in these two articles) it labours to produce, it (he is still talking about the Omnipotent power of the Almighty) is always obliged in the course of its creative effort, to pass through a whole series of intermediaries and to overcome a whole succession of inevitable risks - whatever may

---

[10] Ibid. p. 31.

be said by theologians, who are always ready to introduce the operation of the absolute power of the Divine".

Even if we overlook Teilhard's attack on orthodox theologians, what about 2000 years of the Church's infallible teaching? Where in the whole of Catholic Tradition and in the inspired text of the Bible have we ever been taught what is being declared here: that the existence of God's freely-chosen creation restricts the omnipotent power of God? Since when do creatures "help God create"?

But listen to this!

Quote 11[11]

"We have already recognised (?) a first general law to which God's operation is subjected in so far as it operates outside itself: that, precisely in virtue of its own perfection, it is unable (!) to act in discontinuity with individual natures or out of harmony with the advance of the Whole, - that is, it must (!) operate on the same plane as the secondary causes. This first restriction on the arbitrary manifestation of God's action leads us to a consideration of two more."

Only people who hate God as He revealed Himself can stoop to portray such a caricature of the Almighty, and even have the gall of calling this drivel 'theology'. Teilhard has no room for God in his evolution. 'If He has to be postulated, let us then, right from the start, put Him in His place and effectively muzzle him', is really what he is saying. To maintain that God's perfection is a forcible

---

[11] Ibid. p. 31-32.

restriction on God's power simply because of the existence of participated beings, creatures meant to help Him create, that is, rearrange and unite pre-existing material, (remember, God cannot create *ex nihilo*, from nothing, in Teilhard's evolution) constitutes a grave Sin against the First Commandment: "I am the Lord thy God".

What are these "two more" restrictions on God?

Quote 12 [12]

"First of all, it appears contradictory (to the nature of participated being) (See Note 3) to imagine God creating an isolated thing ... . For now at last we can see that, if God wished to have Christ, then, to launch a complete universe and scatter life with lavish hand was no more than He was obliged to do. Strictly speaking then, is there in all that moves outside God anything else in act today (other than the actualisation of Jesus Christ) for which each fragment of the world is, proximately or distantly, necessary as a necessary means? We need have no hesitation in saying that there is not."

"If God wished to have Christ ..." Such blasphemy! Here we are far removed from Christ, the Second Person of the Blessed Trinity, co-existent with God from all eternity before creation. Even if philosophy wants to speculate about a universe in the pretence that there is no divine Revelation, no such luxury can be given to theol-

---

[12] Ibid. p. 32.

ogy, least of all to Catholic Theology which - as we will see - all this is supposed to be!

Note (3): "... contradictory to the nature of participated being." Never mind, if all this is contradictory to the Nature of God! Teilhard participates in 'creating', and so his nature has to be safeguarded first at the expense of the Divine Nature.

Only for one 'Christ' is the created universe necessary "as a necessary means": the 'cosmic-Christ', that feverish chimera of Teilhard's evolutionary imagination, a non-existing figment of an evil illusion. Since this 'Christ' does not exist, then neither does the necessity for this universe to exist as his receptacle and 'milieu'.

Quote 13[13]

"If the general law of becoming (i.e. the controlling of the progressive appearance of being, created being, from an unorganised multiple) must be regarded as modalities rigourously imposed on God's action, then we can begin to see that the existence of evil might very well also be a strictly inevitable concomitant of creation ... No, we have to accept that in spite of God's power, God cannot obtain a creature united to himself without necessarily engaging in a struggle with some evil. For evil appears inevitably with the first atom of being which creation (!) releases into existence. Creature and sinlessness (absolute and general) are terms whose association is as incompatible with God's power and wisdom as the coupling of creature and oneness."

---

[13] Ibid. p. 32-33.

No wonder that the 'theology' built on the slime of these assertions has no time for Our Blessed Lady and Her Immaculate Conception denied here. Modern catechesis has followed Teilhard's
intolerance for Our Lady as well as for the Church created in Her
Image and Likeness, the Holy Catholic Church.

To sum it all up:

Quote 14[14]

"All of us are in this world caught up in a tangle of evils and de-
terminisms upon which God himself can act only under certain
very precise conditions; and this because there are obstructions
which are essentially part of material things."

All this goes to show that, when Teilhard allows evolution to
rule supreme, and when he states that "to it alone all theories, all
hypotheses, all systems must bow, and which they must satisfy in
order to be thinkable and true" (see Quote 6 above) he literally
means what he says and he has no intention of excluding God,
Catholic Faith and Catholic Dogma: "Dogma must come to mesh
with science" he states in his 1929 paper *The Human Sense*. The
new god of evolution proclaimed by Teilhard appears to be a god
muzzled by evolution and science in order to be "thinkable and
true". It is no longer Our God, the Living God of the Old and New
Testament, the Father of Our Lord and Saviour, Jesus Christ.

Once we know how 'modern man', that pathetic end-product
of a faked evolution, nullifies Revelation and the Supernatural

---

[14] Ibid. p. 34.

simply by letting them operate within a narrow framework of pre-conceived conditions [that is, if they want to operate at all; we can quite happily do without them in Teilhard's new system], it is inevitable that Christ, the Church and the whole of Catholicism too will all be eclipsed by the only rival left: science. It is only through science that They will be allowed to act and act in silence. They are no longer allowed to speak for themselves: Teilhard will speak on their behalf.

In Quote 6 above, we saw "what makes and classifies a 'modern man'". Teilhard continues:

Quote 15[15]

"Man discovers that he is 'nothing else than evolution become conscious of itself', to borrow Julian Huxley's striking expression (the other militant atheist to whom Teilhard left the dissemination of his manuscripts through his last will). It seems to me that our modern minds (!) (because and in as much as they are modern) will never find rest until they settle down to this view. For on this summit, and on this summit alone, are repose and illumination waiting for us."

Quote 16[16]

"because we ARE evolution".

---

[15] *The Phenomenon of Man.* Op.Cit. p.243.
[16] Ibid. p. 246.

Quote 17[17]

"The spirit of research and conquest is the permanent soul of evolution (See Note 4). Man is not the centre of the universe as we thought once in our simplicity but something much more wonderful - the arrow pointing the way to the final unification of the world in terms of life."

So Christ died for arrows ... We baptise something much more wonderful than a human baby: we baptise arrows! We are supposed to be nothing else, nothing more important in our own eyes and in the eyes of Teilhard's 'Catholicism', "than evolution having become conscious of itself"! As pointing arrows, we are only a mute intermediate step to the "final unification", the looming 'personal collective': the AntiChrist prison state as the final glorification of mankind ...

Too harsh? Too severe on Teilhard? Then read on to find out what name and what roll he allocates to these poor "arrows" those 'disposable human beings' only needed to point the way to some grandiose future beyond themselves in which they do not partake.

(Note 4: In our first quote from Teilhard's work we read that Teilhard allocated to his 'god' the honour of being "the soul of the world". Here he has totally forgotten about that by making "the spirit of research and conquest" the soul of evolution, i.e. science, everywhere proclaimed not only as God's equal, but superior.)

---

[17] Ibid. p. 247.

Quote 18[18]

"For the failure that threatens us (Teilhard is speaking here of the great crisis in evolution, finding itself on the threshold, waiting to be pushed from the noosphere into this 'personal collective') to be turned into a success, for the concurrence of human monads to come about, it is necessary and sufficient for us that we should extend our science to its farthest limits and discover Omega."

"Human monads" Disposable human beings.

So that is the name and the roll Teilhard allocates to his "arrows". Being a monad, a disposable human being, makes "man much more wonderful" than being created in the image and likeness of God.

Remember those millions of Russian, Baltic, Polish, Hungarian, Tchechish, Vietnamese, Tibetan, Chinese, Cambodian "human monads"? Driven to 'concurrence and collectivism' at the point of a gun? No failure there!

'The concurrence of human monads' is equivalent to 'the success of evolution'. This global concurrence of human monads into one collective prison existence is the only way that "the threatened failure of evolution turns into a huge success" ...

No wonder that Mussolini, Hitler, Stalin, Mao-tsetung and any other dictator were worthy of Teilhard's admiration. They dared to push evolution over the threshold of the noosphere into the 'final unification' involving millions of "human monads": disposable human beings.

---

[18] Ibid. p. 294.

So this whole future, this pushing humanity into collectivism, can be safely left to science in its attempts to discover another figment of the Teilhardian imagination, that non-existing 'Omega Point' at the expense of millions of human monads who will never benefit from this 'discovery'.

How long can we give Modernists, Marxists, Satanists and science a free hand before we realise that they know that 'Omega Point' does not exist, and that they don't care two hoots about it anyhow? But now that Teilhard has made us aware of this 'threshold' between the noosphere and the collective, that is, between free individuals and Socialist slaves under One-World government, it is according to our evolutionist masters inevitable that we cross it, if necessary at bayonet point. The Church may as well go along with that or else wither away and be left behind, as he so eloquently develops in *The Human Sense* (1929), his most vicious attack on the Mother Church and his formal break with Her:

Quote 19[19]

"Let us be honest. At bottom the Church has never understood as we do today, the beautiful human spirit nor the sacred passion for research, those two fundamental elements of modern thought. No matter what glosses one puts on it: the *Syllabus of Errors* was an effort to condemn the most solid of present-day hopes. After that how could Man continue to love the Church and to respect her?"

---

[19] *The Human Sense.* See remarks made in (3) above.

The 80 Propositions of His Holiness Pope Pius IX, issued on Dec. 8, 1864, commonly known as *The Syllabus of Errors* and held up to ridicule here by Teilhard, was meant to prevent his type of thinking from getting a foothold in the Holy Catholic Church. With Teilhard de Chardin's open demand to consider it abolished we can hear the audible sigh of relief in Hell and the 'Hear, Hear' in the wings of the global 'scientific' theatre. Top Humanists and Socialists don't believe in evolution nor in a papal *Syllabus of Errors*. Like their more ruthless blood-brothers the Communists, they simply believe in the power that comes out of the barrel of a gun and from repressive legislation.

But they will passionately promote this type of thinking amongst Catholics, and will financially support every school, seminary, Catholic teachers college and catechetical ventures where the abolition of the Syllabus in favour of evolution will be taught and disseminated, and this for obvious reasons.!

Nowhere in Teilhard's writings is there room for the Catholic Church unless to knock Her. As he wrote himself: he is disillusioned with the Catholic Church. With the next quote from his 1929 paper *The Human Sense*, he finally and irrevocably turned his back on Her:

Quote 20[20]

"The Church no longer gives the impression of 'thinking with humanity'. Such is the profound reason for the atmosphere of hos-

---

[20] Ibid.

tility and disdain that floats around her. And such is also the explanation for her present sterility. .... No one has ever been able to rekindle a love that has burned out ...."

There is no room for Her in his completely self-sufficient system. Evolution takes care of everything and the Church can only hamper this progress. Modern 'religion' can only be the religion of an entirely new 'church', an anti-church, the church of 'modern man', according to this genius so misunderstood by the Catholic Church.

But what did His Holiness Pope St. Pius X have to say, when he clearly foresaw and described for us this One-World 'Church of Darkness'? When he told us how it would be conceived in, and born from, dark workshops in which are elaborated these mischievous doctrines which ought not to seduce clear-thinking minds?

This is what he wrote in his Motu Proprio *Our Apostolic Mandate* of 1910:

"What has become of their Catholicity?' asks the Holy Father And then he answers his own question: "Alas, it is now no more than a miserable affluent feeding the great movement of apostasy organised in every country for the establishment of a One-World Church, which shall have neither dogma nor hierarchy, neither discipline for the mind nor curb on the passions, and which, under the pretext of freedom and human dignity, would bring back to the world the reign of legalised cunning and brute force, and the oppression of the weak, and of all those who toil and suffer".

What sort of a 'church' is that? If that turns out to be some kind of global agglomerate as this Saint predicted it would be, then it can only come from something so totally wrong but so universally accepted as only "another gospel" can be "which they thought was the true Gospel of Jesus Christ" (ibid.). We can only point to one system strong enough, central as well as global enough, deceptive as well as disobedient enough to claim full responsibility for the actual introduction of this fatal 'church of darkness'. It is the system discussed in these pages: the relentless and systematic introduction, acceptance, dissemination and implementation of the theories and practices of Teilhard de Chardin in the hope that under its faked 'freedom of conscience' Catholics would at last be allowed to let go of the Cross and, in his evolutionary system, take his 'armchair ride to God'.

His appeal amongst Catholics was global and instant, so it simply had to be Catholic doctrine. This near unanimity could only come from the Holy Spirit. It couldn't be otherwise. The Church had to be wrong in resisting the light that shone forth from this 'genius'. But was She? If the foregoing was pretty convincing that She was NOT, listen to the rest of the story:

Quote 21 [21]

"Just as in living bodies one cell, at first similar to the others, can gradually come to be preponderant in the organism, so the particular humanity of Christ was able, at least at the Resurrection, to take on and to acquire a universal morphological function."

To Teilhard even Redemption is biological, scientific, evolutionary. This becomes clear from the use of the word 'morphologi-

---

[21] *Christianity and Evolution.* Op. Cit., p. 41. Fall, Redemption & Geocentrism, 1920.

cal', and from the ordinary meaning he attaches to this term. For this we refer to another article of the same year (1920), to the one in which he denies the possibility of miracles, in which he states:

Quote 22[22]

"On the other hand we have no example even in legend of a morphological miracle ...."

Legend?? Myth?? Folklore?? Gospel??

... to which he attaches the following footnote:

"e.g. the restoration of a limb." (Note by Fr. Teilhard).

With this footnote Teilhard informs us that, in his writings, 'morphological' retains its ordinary, biological meaning. So when he writes - as we saw - that especially after the Resurrection Christ's humanity acquires a universal, morphological function, then he wants us to understand that in the ordinary biological meaning. Anyhow, the purely biological function of Christ's Humanity in the Kingdom of God is spelled out explicitly in *The Phenomenon of Man*:

Quote 23[23]

"Is the Kingdom of God a big family? he asks. Yes in a sense it is. But in another sense it is a prodigious BIOLOGICAL operation, that is, of the Redeeming Incarnation."

---

[22] Ibid. 'Notes on the modes .. etc.', p. 29.

[23] *The Phenomenon of Man*. Op.Cit., p.321.

So at last here it is in full view. That which, according to Catholic Dogma, he should still be teaching but refuses to teach: namely that it is Original Sin which is passed on through sexual propagation, that is, through a prodigious biological function, that he now transfers to Redemption, making it a morphological, biological function, and a prodigious one at that, in his self-sufficient but equally self-destructive, non-existent evolutionary system.

What a boon for modern 'catechesis': 'Redemption' passed on through SEX! (Remember the warning of Pope St. Pius X? "No Curb on the Passions in the 'Church of Darkness'"!)

Maybe as a last resort (and we are now clutching at straws) will Teilhard allow 'love' to pierce the infernal shell around his evolutionary treadmill, so that the "human monads" captivated in his suffocating 'church of darkness' will be able to escape before the whole system closes in on them like a trap. Will he permit the poor monads who wish to get out an escape through 'love'?

Quote 24[24]

"Love in all its subtleties is nothing more, and nothing less, than the more or less direct trace marked on the heart of the element by the psychical convergence of the universe upon itself."

Whatever that means, it does not look very inviting as an 'escape route'. A universe converging upon itself has all the ominous overtones of a gigantic vortex sucking up and crushing everything that crosses its path.

---

[24] Ibid. p. 291.

Better steer clear of love in that system!

And so spiritually starved and emaciated human monads are to remain trapped forever in this suffocating hell of the Teilhardian 'church of darkness' unless ...

Unless an expedition is mounted, and free agents, truly Marian and papal Catholics, come to the rescue ...

Section II

Which deals with the for orthodox Catholics important question: "Has the foregoing truly been declared to be Catholic Theology?"

In the course of the research into this whole matter, three witnesses will be called up and their testimonies examined.

They are:

N. M. Wildiers, *Docteur en Théologie* and Prof. of Theology.
Walter M. Abbott, S.J.
J. P. Kenny, S.J.

As already stated, this Section II will examine whether Teilhard's system has in all seriousness been called Catholic Theology, and if so, whether this claim has extended far enough for us to worry about its infiltration into Catholic schools.

These questions are gravely important because not only is Teilhard's system diametrically opposed to Divine Revelation, but as we saw, he has made his 'sex education' an integral part of that 'theology', and so Teilhard's 'sex teachings' are diametrically opposed to Divine Revelation and to two thousand years of Catholic Tradition.

The double question posed here will be answered with three quotations, but they are of the utmost importance and most revealing.

As a first witness I call before the Bar of History Professor N. Wildiers, *Docteur en Théologie*, and himself also a Professor of Theology.

This man saw fit to write the following Foreword to *Christianity and Evolution*, a motley assortment of Teilhard's privately circulated papers.

"Whatever reservations one may have about the decision (to make a selection out of the welter of Teilhardian papers available) we feel nevertheless that the selection presented in this volume has the advantage of bringing out with equal clarity both the theoretical and practical aspects of the author's theological thought. In recent years much has been published about Teilhard de Chardin's theological writings, both about his theology as a whole and about particular points in his teaching (Note 5). Seldom in the history of theology has a writer's thought been the occasion, in so few years, of so much, often passionate, study and discussion. The number and the quality of the studies devoted to his work in this field make it abundantly clear how insistently Pere Teilhard's thought has captivated the attention of theologians, and what an unusually powerful stimulus it is to the theological speculation of our day."

(Note 5. *"his teachings"*. Teilhard's *'teachings'* were given out in grave disobedience, since he had been forbidden to teach by the Church since 1926, reinforced in 1947.)

And then, at the end of his Foreword, Prof. Wildiers gives us an unexpected bonus in answering the un-spoken question in the minds of many:

> "Apart from Christological questions, most of the essays in this volume deal primarily with the problem of Original Sin. Any informed reader will realise that what he will find are essays which Teilhard intended and hoped would be examined more closely by professional theologians. While some of his suggestions may still seem somewhat tentatively expressed, there can nevertheless be little doubt that it is in the direction he indicates that theological research on this issue is being pursued."

So there it is straight from the horse's mouth: if the interest in Teilhard's 'theology' is as worldwide as this man would like us to believe it is, and if this worldwide theological research is being pursued in the direction of Teilhard's rejection of the Dogma of Original Sin (both his 1922 and 1947 papers are in this edition), and if professional theologians now treat Teilhard's audacity as *'suggestions somewhat tentatively put'*, then we have here a clear description of the foundations on which the so-called 'Catholic part' of the One-World 'Church of Darkness' has been built. It can only be based on heresy and deception of this nature and magnitude.

My second witness before the Bar of History to testify to acceptance of Teilhard's ideas as a 'theology' and to the worldwide influence it commands is Walter M. Abbott S.J. His testimony is found in a *footnote* in the edition of *The Documents of Vatican II* of which he is the Editor. It is on p. 269 in the middle of the *Pastoral Constitution on The Church in the Modern World*. In order to appreciate the 'non sequitur' of the footnote, i.e. in order to show that this footnote most certainly does not follow from the text of the Council document, I will first quote here the relevant Conciliar text:

"May the faithful therefore live in very close union with the men of their time. Let them strive to understand perfectly their way of thinking and feeling as expressed in their culture. Let them blend modern science and its theories and the understanding of its most recent discoveries with Christian morality and doctrine. Thus their religious practice and morality can keep pace with their scientific knowledge and with technology."

All this is of course perfectly natural and orthodox, and could have been written by anyone at any time of the Church's long history of evangelisation; by anyone that is who takes an interest in his brother and who has his eternal salvation at heart. One does not have to be a Teilhard de Chardin, one does not have to reject Original Sin, adopt a philosophy built on severe contradictions and embrace evolution-as-fact in order to put into practice what the Council here recommends.

Nowhere does the Council state, as Teilhard stipulates, that the Church's doctrine and morality must come to '*mesh*' with modern science: quite the reverse, as is to be expected! Yet this is what Fr. Abbott's footnote has to offer 'by way of explanation':

"Here as elsewhere it is easy to recognise the compatibility of insights by thinkers such as Teilhard de Chardin in his '*Divine Milieu*' (Note 6) (Harper, 1960) with the fundamental outlook of the Council. In a sense, this statement of the Constitution ratifies the basic inspiration of the 'nouvelle théologie' of the 1940's. For those familiar with some of the controversy over the 'nouvelle théologie' at the time, it may be of interest to note that several of its leading promoters, including Fathers Henri de Lubac S.J., Jean Daniélou S.J. and Yves Congar O.P. served as expert consultants (periti) to the commission responsible for drafting this Constitution".

(Note 6. Like everyone else who had an intense interest in seeing Teilhard accepted by the Church's Magisterium, Fr. Abbott knew that for 40 years (since 1926) and for very good reasons Rome had rejected outright giving an Imprimatur to Teilhard's most important book: *Le Milieu Divin*. Here Fr. Abbott introduces into a Council document the rejected contents of this book as fundamental to an understanding of the whole of Vatican II and the 'new theology'.)

So here we are told, not only that '*la nouvelle théologie*' is in fact Teilhardian, but that the influence of Teilhard as a theologian is so phenomenal that his view is the fundamental outlook of the whole Council, and so of the whole of Catholicism after Vatican II! If that is not assigning to Teilhard as a theologian a worldwide influence, then I wouldn't know what is. How anyone can read into the sober paragraph of the above-quoted Council document (1) a fundamentally Teilhardian outlook (2) underlying the whole Council; or who can see in it (3) the ratification by the whole Church of a totally new and controversial 'theology', as well as (4) the approval of a book rejected by the Church for more than 40 years, defies com-prehension!

By now the conclusion is becoming inescapable: if Teilhard is such a poor theologian, but his influence is so worldwide that the greatest names in Catholic theology are falling over each other to adopt his fundamental insights and system and to develop them into a new theology, then Teilhard can only be seen as a flag, an excuse, to cover a secret and totally forbidden cargo to be brought inside the Catholic Church. His powerful followers must have had ulterior motives before, during and after the Council in changing the whole of Catholic Philosophy and Theology. It was *they* who wanted a new faith, a faith that would one day unite the whole world in a new church of inter-communion, the One-World Church foreseen by Pope St. Pius X, a 'Church of Darkness'. But in order that this could be done, they had to implement first what this Holy Pontiff had predicted, with Divine precision, would be need-ed for that:

"They have been carried away to 'another gospel' which they thought was the true Gospel of Jesus Christ."

How truly prophetic that was! For overnight the insanity of the modernist 'gospel' of Teilhard de Chardin, with its strained lan-guage and garbled utterances, provided them with the blueprint they had been looking for and which they could read perfectly! Thus it was that they, and they alone, who became the architects of this new One-World Church of Inter-Communion, rejecting from their plans the living stones of the One True Church created in the image and likeness of the Holy Virgin Mary, Mother of God!

If a third testimony is needed, although anaemic as befitting the pen of one of Melbourne's dimmer lights, Fr. J. P. Kenny S.J., then here it is. It has its function here.

For just as the previous witness tried to convince us that 'the whole Church is Teilhardian' because of Vatican II, so this 'teacher' of seminarians by day and of Christians by night tries to tell us that the whole Church is Teilhardian because of the Pope. If this Fr. Kenny really believes what he writes, then he is *approximate to heresy* according to an official assessment made of his contributions to a series of 'Catholic-Presbyterian' discussions, initiated in the late sixties by Archbishop James Knox.

In *The Advocate*, the one-time Catholic weekly of the Melbourne Archdiocese, Fr. Kenny wrote a review of a book on Original Sin in the issue of July 6, 1972. The book was written by a French theologian, Fr. Henri Rondet. Apart from the fact that the erroneous tenets of this review run counter to Trent (Denz . Sch. 1511), Holy Scripture (Rom. 5:12) and Tradition echoed by Pope Paul VI (Credo), the heretical implications made here are, that a personal sin of Adam is not Revealed Truth, is not Defined Truth, can be relegated to oblivion, and is still subject to dispute and argument.

The tone of the review is such that the official teaching of the Church is held up to ridicule and contempt for being rather timid and backward. Here is a quote from the review:

> "Rondet is a positive scholar, certainly not a creative thinker of the calibre of Rahner, Teilhard de Chardin or Congar. Something much bolder than Rondet's rather timorous and

backward looking attempt is needed *if a theologian is going to reformulate the Dogma of Original Sin* (<u>where did we hear that phrase before</u>?) along the lines mapped out by Vatican II or Pope Paul ..."

And then follows part of a speech by Pope Paul VI which, as can be expected, has nothing whatsoever to do with the reformulation of the Dogma of Original Sin.

Once again, the name of Teilhard is freely linked with the teachings of the Second Vatican Council and so with the whole post-conciliar renewal, to convey the impression that his influence is worldwide and universally accepted by the greatest names in Catholic theology. To quote the Holy Father here as being on the side of the heresies of Teilhard de Chardin is a gratuitous insult. It runs counter to the teachings of Pope Paul VI's famous (but never quoted) *Credo of the People of God.*

We can now be satisfied that research in these matters is absolutely essential. Teilhard's teaching has been officially called a 'theology', 'the new theology'. It has provoked a worldwide interest and all the great names in Catholic theology are proudly supporting his thoughts and developing his ideas. And notwithstanding a consistent attitude of rejection and warning, the Catholic Church is held up (even as we saw in the most orthodox of documents) as having adopted his fundamental outlook. And finally, we have been repeatedly assured that the main thrust of 'the New Theology' is in the direction opened up by Teilhard's rejection of the Dogma of Original Sin as taught and understood by the Universal Church.

The remaining space of this short essay could be conveniently spent on a more energetic probing below the surface so to speak, in order to get a firmer grip on the evil of 'Teilhardism', that is, an intellectual hold of the deadly substance of the injection which has remained even (as seems to be the case) 'syringe Teilhard' is being quietly discarded now that all the 'great names' have achieved their goal.

Section III

"The Root-Cause of "Teilhardism."

A brief research into the fundamental flaw and fallacy underlying all Teilhard de Chardin's writings.

Every Theology presupposes a Philosophy from which it is presented with the 'first Principles' of its research. If the Philosophy of *St. Thomas Aquinas,* the *Philosophia Perennis* or *Everlasting Philosophy* had adequately expressed Teilhard's views and 'synthesis', there would never have been any reason for him and his followers to cast around for another philosophy. If the 'Real Distinction' of the Philosophy of St. Thomas Aquinas between God and the created universe had been the fundamental principle or 'starting point' for Teilhard, he would have remained a Thomist. As it was he hated Thomism, for it would not allow him to throw away **real distinctions, absolutes** and **objective reality**.

Right from the beginning Teilhard set out on the *theological plane,* ignoring philosophy. His theological speculations came first, and his First World War was with Catholic Dogma. Since he was quite fixed in his mind what he wanted on that 'plane', he set out to fabricate his own 'philosophy' in support of his faulty, untested 'theology'. This is not only totally unacceptable: it is totally impossible, and in such a 'system' neither 'philosophy' nor 'theology' make any sense, which has remained God's vengeance with all those who followed Teilhard in tampering with Catholic Dogma.

If we follow his groping through his earlier work (1922), we see how desperate he is to formulate his first or fundamental requirement or 'insight': the *a priori* <u>theological</u> *'wish of sameness'* between God and creation (we can't speak of a 'view' here!). It was only an afterthought that this called for a secondary requirement: a <u>philosophical</u> *'wish of identity'* between two contradictories, which he could not possibly hope to get from Thomism, but which he found in 'evolution'.

It never worried him that there was no proof for evolution, nor that he himself never attempted to provide that proof. It never worried him that his 'system' was full of contradictions, which *Dietrich von Hildebrand* so shrewdly observed and wrote down in his famous 'Appendix' to his book *Trojan Horse in the City of God*:

> *"I do not know of another thinker who so artfully jumps from one position to another contradictory one, without being disturbed by the jump or even noticing it...."*

In Teilhard's view the identity between 'godhead' and universe over the extended humanity of Christ was so absolutely necessary that evolution simply had to be true! If the universe was evolving, then the 'godhead' simply had to evolve with it. Clear thinking, objective reality, contradictions and distinctions, as demanded by Thomism, simply didn't come in to it! His system *had to be right*, anything that clashed with it had to be wrong. "Dogma has to come to mesh with science." (*The Human Sense*, 1929).

Of Thomism the Popes have written:

"In view of all this it is not surprising that the Church will have her future Priests brought up on the Philosophy which derives its method, its system and its basic principles from the Angelic Doctor. [St. Thomas]. One thing is clearly established by the long experience of the ages: his teaching seems to chime in, by a kind of pre-established harmony, with Divine Revelation. No surer way to safeguard the First Principles of the Faith." (*Humani Generis*, 1950).

This makes a lot of things quite clear. It means that any contradictory system will have no harmony with Divine Revelation, will never chime in with it and will not safeguard the First Principles of Catholic Faith. We only have to look at the unbelievable bankruptcy of Catholic thinking all around us to appreciate just how widespread the acceptance of a contradictory system has become. Any so-called 'theology' that rejects a Dogma of the Faith will never rise to the status of a true theology, since it will never touch on Divine Revelation, and so will never study it, which is the most profound task that theology can set itself.

What is it then, that Teilhard tries to describe in his *Milieu Divin*? It is this. To him, the Hypostatic Union, which is the union between the Word of God, the Second Person of the Blessed Trinity, and His human nature, must be extended to the whole of creation. This makes to the author and to all his followers the whole of the universe essentially divine, since it has the same function for the 'cosmic-Christ' as the Sacred Humanity had for Christ as we know Him. It 'divinises' His new 'humanity': *us*.

Christ in His Sacred Humanity could not sin, so we, in the 'sacred humanity' (divine milieu) of the 'cosmic-Christ' also cannot sin. The whole idea of 'sin' is to be banned forever, right from its origin: **Original Sin!**

And just as Christ could grow in His Sacred Humanity from Child to Manhood, so humanity in the 'cosmic-Christ' can grow through the various stages of evolution, to 'omega point'. The created universe is now the 'divine milieu': there is no need for the Supernatural as a separate 'layer'. The 'cosmic-Christ' embraces all that. In him we are all essentially divinised. Matter is sacred, 'divine', because it is the 'sacred humanity' of the 'cosmic-Christ', his body in time and space.

Here on earth the Church (if She behaves, and follows the 'party line') may be said to embody ideally what his body in time and space ought to be, but there is no longer an *essential* difference between Catholic and non-Catholic, since all are part of the 'cosmic-Christ'. To Teilhard the Church is only a model, but not necessarily the best model, to be accepted by all, and a model subject to science.

With this we have hit on the rock-bottom of the great schism and confusion of our days. It is precisely here where the Catholic Church and the Teilhardian 'church of darkness' part company. To Teilhard, evolution ends up *inevitably* in 'god-omega'. To Catholics, inevitability of salvation was NEVER part of Catholic doctrine or Tradition. To Teilhard, the whole of 'reality' is nothing but an arm-chair ride to God. And the soft Western Catholics who embraced evolution so they could hang on to their wealth without being embarrassed by God or conscience, are letting themselves be tempted to let go of the Cross, and with a sigh of relief, they sit back and are letting themselves be carried to God in the embrace of this evolutionary church. They even have armchairs for Mass in many chapels and churches!

It is in this whole evolutionary mess that Catholics are taught to stop worrying about Sin and about the eternal salvation of themselves and others as well: we all end up in God!

It is here that the Catholic Church becomes utterly superfluous. It is here that the Catholic Church is being told to stop all Her previous missionary activities; to concentrate Her efforts on 'liberation theology' and social justice, and only bring the glorious ideas of the new Christianity and the 'cosmic-Christ' to others, so that they too can take part in this pleasure cruise, this armchair ride to Heaven.

It is here that we find the Teilhardian influence as the basis of the rampant false ecumenism, which thrives on the suppression of yet another Dogma of the Catholic Faith: *the Uniqueness of the Catholic Church* and of the Catholic Faith within Her; the one true Church founded by Christ and absolutely necessary for the salvation of all. This never meant that everybody has to be a Catholic, but only that the graces for everybody's salvation come exclusively from and through the unique Catholic Church, Head and members.

To Teilhard, Christ was always 'the soul of evolution', becoming more 'Christ' as time went on, and at a given instant he 'pierced through the envelope' and became visible, to show us how to help him evolve to perfection. Evolution then, not Christ's Church, appears to be the ultimate reality of everything and the fundamental dogma embracing all there is to know. To all Teilhardian Marxists and Catholics alike, all concepts and ideas centre around this fundamental postulate: that of evolution having, through Teilhard, become conscious of itself and so having become 'personalised'. As Von Hildebrand so accurately grasped in his *Trojan Horse in the City of God*: Teilhardians make 'awareness of oneself' the criterium for 'becoming a person'. If through Teilhard and his innumerable followers, evolution has become aware of itself and so has become personalised, not in an individual sense, but in a mass sense, then this means we have reached the superior state of the 'personal collective': the dream of every communist, socialist and humanist.

How does Thomism define 'personhood'? To a Thomist a *person* is someone who *possesses* him/herself, which of necessity implies two things. One, that a person knows him/herself to be clearly distinct from all that one is *not*. And two, if objective existence must be given to oneself as a person, then the same objective reality must be granted to all the other persons and to everything else from which each person is distinct.

Thus, there exists an essential relationship with objective reality and with all that goes with it, which is denied in Teilhard's 'personal collective'.

It is true that many Priests nowadays who believe in all sorts of contradictions: who believe in 'women priests', 'married priests', the false ecumenism; who believe in means of salvation outside the Catholic Church and who no longer care, really, what they believe; and no longer can tell the difference between Catholic Faith and any other 'Christian faith': it is true that they are not Teilhardian in the sense that they believe in a 'god' evolving with the universe. But they believe in evolution and in the reformulation of some Dog-

mas, and they have embraced in practice THE most essential Teilhardian 'dogma' of '*La Nouvelle Théologie*': the inevitability of Salvation, with or without evolution. And so they may as well be
called "Teilhardians' ...

Section IV

"Final Summing-up and Conclusions"

So much then for the 'fundamental theological insights' of Pierre Teilhard de Chardin S.J. which, so they tell us,

- form the foundation for *La Nouvelle Théologie*,
- were approved and adopted by Vatican II,
- have captured the attention of theologians,
- have become 'an unusual, powerful stimulus' to the theological speculation of our days,
- have pointed to the direction in which theological research is being pursued,
- and which the Church 'misunderstood and wrongly resisted' with Her 1962 *Monita*.

These were the 'theological teachings' of Teilhard as expressed in his numerous papers, which were freely circulated and discussed in many of the Jesuit Houses of Higher Study for 35 years: from the early twenties to 1955, the year of his death, and ever since.

No one can possibly deny that the 20-odd quotes selected in this paper look ugly when held up against the light.

No one can possibly maintain that they are genuine Catholic teaching.

And no one can deny that they come from Teilhard.

It can be safely asserted that the untold damage, caused by the adoption of this nonsense as genuine theological insights, came about not so much through Teilhard himself, as through global, corporate disobedience of his uncritical followers in discarding known Church teaching. Maybe there could be some Jesuits now who would privately agree with the substance of this paper that Teilhardism is untenable. Maybe there are by now some, who would look upon Teilhardism as on a useless syringe, discarded after the deadly poison had been injected into the bloodstream of the Church. Maybe in time we may even hear that expressed a bit more publicly and forcefully.

But at the moment it is still fully true that, what looked from the outside such a pleasant, ecumenical cruise-ship, such a welcome change from the storm-tossed Barque of St. Peter, appeared, on closer examination, to be nothing but a slave-trader. Once on board, you are not being taken to 'Omega Point', you are being directly ferried to a concentration camp: to a dark church with no dogma and no hierarchy, with no discipline of the mind or curb on the passions. Your destiny is the full reign of legalised cunning and brute force, of the oppression of the weak and of all those who toil and suffer. It is not a 'church' these slaves are being taken to, but through the endless misery of loss of Catholic Faith, to a place of outer darkness: a dungeon.

May all the Catholics who preferred to remain on board the Barque of St. Peter en route to their Father's House, bless their good fortune, and realise the utter calamity of being a Teilhardian!

And may the anguished cry of Our Blessed Lady at Fatima not be in vain:

"Pray, pray a great deal and make sacrifices. Many souls go to Hell because there is no one to pray or to makes sacrifices for them". (July 13, 1917)

Book IV

Tradition

Frits Albers, Ph.B.
(October 13, 1979)

Preface

Many good Catholics, steeped in Tradition, who have so far managed to keep the Faith as it was handed down to them from the Apostles, are often accused of drawing their strength from pre-Vatican II sources. This accusation implies the charge that they behave as if Vatican II never took place, or that they missed its unique message for the Church of our times.

The proper defense against such allegations is, of course, for these good Catholics to maintain, that if they cannot agree with their adversaries on the meaning and validity of the pre-Vatican II Catholic Church, it is entirely futile to discuss with them the place and inspiration of the Second Vatican Council. True Catholicism rightly maintains, that the voice of Pope Pius XII has the same ring of authority for our times as it had for the post-war era of the world of his own time. That the teachings of the Great Councils of the Church are guiding and stabilizing the Church of our times as much as the Church of the future.

If Vatican II is to be accepted as one of those great Councils in the history of the Catholic Church, then it must, on close scrutiny, reveal to us that it speaks with the same Voice that was heard through the centuries, and that it passes on to us, and beyond us, the same Deposit of Faith, that was entrusted to the Church initially, the guardianship of which has been the sole prerogative of the Living Magisterium within the Catholic Church, infallibly assisted herewith by the Holy Spirit.

"Christ is the same, yesterday, today, forever."

Yet, each Council of the Church has been unique ... For our solid Catholics it must be heartening to notice that the uniqueness of Vatican II does not lie where the noisy Teilhardian and Marxist 'Catholics' have been protesting for years that it is to be found:

- ❖ In a break with the pre-Vatican II Church of Tradition.
- ❖ In a break with the Church that gave us Trent and a Pope Pius IX.
- ❖ In a break with the Church of the *Syllabus* and *Pascendi*.
- ❖ In a break with a Church that dared to declare Anglican Orders invalid.
- ❖ In a break with the Church of Lourdes: its miracles and great devotion to Our Lady.
- ❖ In a break with the Church of Fatima and the Holy Rosary.
- ❖ In a break with the Church of Dogmas and Anathemas.

So great is the acute disappointment of the modernists with Vatican II, so minimal are the '*concessios*' they could squeeze out of its uniqueness, that they have altogether scotched their erstwhile fierce attempts to trace all their frightful heresies to Her documents, and are now forced, in the face of mounting resistance against their absurd claims to continuity, to prepare for their own 'council': a future council in their very own 'church of darkness'.

Yes, Vatican II is unique. But its uniqueness shares in the Mystery of the Church: that great Mystery that surrounds all God's Revelation and Truth entrusted to His Church: impregnable and closed for 'the proud in the conceit of their heart', yet open to 'the

poor in spirit, and understood and accepted by children, the children of Mary'.

   To all these little ones who are at present scandalised by the
make-believe that Teilhardism and Modernism and Marxism make
up 'the new Catholic church' of our times ensuing from Vatican II,
these few pages are humbly dedicated. May their supernatural, un-
worldly resistance to this poison: injected 'into the heart and veins
of the Catholic Church by those whose capacity to injure Her is the
surer because their knowledge of Her is the more intimate' (Pope
St. Pius X in *Pascendi*) confound their enemies, and please God, in
time to convert their torturers.

Introduction

In this Introduction I will endeavor to put the subject-matter of the whole article in context and perspective.

Tradition is the ultimate weapon ... It is God's Word, handed down through the ages:

> "alive and powerful, penetrating deeper than any two-edged sword ... quick to distinguish every thought and design in our hearts." (Hebr. 4:12).

Tradition, then, will uncover every thought and design in the heart of a modernist. The Voice of Tradition will finally identify the cockle from the wheat. **Tradition**, not colourful photographs, will decide if a Bishop is still 'in communion with Rome'. It is before the Bar of **Tradition** that once and for all the question will be settled: 'which interpretation of Vatican II is authentic'. For the Voice of **Tradition** is inseparable from the voice of God in Holy Writ: infallible.

Far from acting, as our detractors would have us do, as if Vatican II never took place, we will drag their own creation: 'the church of darkness' before the Judgement seat of **Tradition**. And there we will hold it up against the Light of Vatican II in exactly the same way as Christ held up the false tradition of the Sanhedrin against that very same Light: Himself, before the judgement seat of Pilate.

We will then, for the moment, ignore the mounting blasphemies, obscenities and heresies which are being passed on everywhere as the 'new Catholic insights', just as Christ ignored in silence the mounting riot that was gathering all around Him in His Sacred Passion, clamoring in the end for His crucifixion. With Him we will concentrate on His Bride, our suffering Mother, the Holy Catholic Church, before, during and after Vatican II, and wrestle like Jacob, to come to grips with the magnitude of the Reality that God has reserved in His Wisdom for our time.

That the matter of Tradition is of overriding importance, is based on solid evidence contained in Holy Writ. In the First Book of Maccabees we read the following:

> "It was then that there emerged from Israel a set of renegades who led many people astray. 'Come', they said, '**let us reach an understanding with the Pagans surrounding us**; for since we separated ourselves from them, many misfortunes have overtaken us'. This proposal proved acceptable, and a number of the people eagerly approached the king, who authorised them to practice the pagan observances. So they built a gymnasium in Jerusalem, such as the pagans have, **disguised their circumcision** and abandoned the Holy Covenant, submitting to the heathen rule as willing slaves of impiety."

What is stated here has such an obvious parallel with our present-day situation, that we should not be surprised if, in the Providence of God, the whole of the Books of Maccabees has a bearing on our own tribulations and deliverance.

1. The first thing to notice here is, that the sacred author teaches us to identify the enemy, and call him enemy: rene-

gade! To be truthful in such important matters pertaining to the Faith is therefore not being uncharitable. The biblical reference here "who led many astray", not only shows, that identifying cockle as cockle is not uncharitable: it shows the true basis of the teaching of the great St. Thomas Aquinas:

> "Because an irrational patience sows vice, nurtures neglect, and not only invites bad people to evil, but also the good ones." (ST: IIa, IIae, Q 158, Art 8).

2. Next, the sacred author make us realise that, just as in the period he describes, Hellenism was not to be considered a new, modern, inspired and exciting interpretation of the true Jewish Tradition, neither are Teilhardism and Modernism in our days. Teilhard too, in his endeavours 'to come to an understanding with the non-Catholic world around us', makes out as if that world has progress on its side, and as if Catholicism has been left behind. He even goes so far as to use the very words of the renegades just quoted, not only to blame the Catholic Church for the separation, but to state that it was the Catholic Church who separated itself from the rest of the world, and that this is precisely the cause of the misfortunes that have plagued the Church since.

Here are some of his words, taken from his most bitter article against the Catholic Church, containing his formal break with Her: *The Human Sense* 1929.

Selected Works of Frits Albers on Pierre Teilhard de Chardin, S.J.

"[4] The Christian Conflict and the Religion of the Future. Faith in the world is inserting itself irresistibly at the heart of a civilisation still dominated – or at least historically formed – by faith in Christ. It is inevitable that a very grave organic struggle should arise from the meeting of these two principles. Perception of this profound drama yields a very clear explanation of the troubles that have been besetting the world of established religions in the west for a hundred years.

Growing Indifference of Men toward Christianity. Christianity has become antipathetic to man. The Christian religion seems narrow to our spirit and our hearts suffocate in it. And why is that? Precisely because it has not yet made room for, because it even gives the impression of opposing the aspirations of the human sense. The Human Sense believes in the magnificent future of the tangible world, the Gospel seems to disdain it. Between the Gospel of the Encyclicals and the Human Sense there exists at present a deep discord. Humanity today believes in the World; the Church of Christ does not wish to believe therein. The Church no longer gives the impression of 'thinking with humanity'. Such is the profound reason for the atmosphere of hostility and disdain which floats around her. And such is also the explanation for her present sterility ... The Christian can try to persuade himself that he still believes in the Primacy of the Fall, the expiation by Christ and the scorn of temporal things. Already he is forcing himself, and also he is falsifying himself. No one has ever been able to rekindle a love that has burned out ... Let us be honest: when all is said and done, the Church has never understood as we do today, the

beautiful human spirit ... After that, how can a Christian continue to love and respect Her."

Sad reading. In December 1971, the American magazine
Triumph printed in full, for the first time, Teilhard's *The Human Sense*, to expose to all for the salvation of souls, the real
Teilhard: the renegade. No one before had dared to print it in
full for fear of giving the game away. Even now only an emasculated version has appeared in English in *Teilhard de Chardin.
Toward the Future*. Collins, 1975. But that is still devastating
enough. The essay bears a striking resemblance to the words
spoken by the renegades in the above quoted passage from
Maccabees: how the Church is now accused of deliberately and
obstinately keeping Herself away from the World (according to
St. James, She should keep Herself spotless and undefiled from
this world), is thereby separating Herself entirely from humanity, is left behind by humanity, and now has only Herself to
blame for the misfortunes that have befallen Her since ...

3. The third thing to observe in this passage of Sacred Scripture
is the <u>action</u> taken by these renegades: they take pains in hiding the
fullness and integrity of their original loyalty. In our days (as Teilhard so eloquently expressed above) these same people are
ashamed of the Catholic Church and of their own Catholicity.
They want to be known as 'Christians'. They want all the
protestants, the pagans, the scientists and the atheists to know how
close they are to them in their world-view. And since they keep on
telling us *ad nauseam* that 'they are the church' they want to create
the impression for the benefit of all the outsiders, that the whole

church has accepted Teilhard's correction, and has now adopted his new way of looking at things since Vatican II.

4. 'But God had other thoughts ...'

The Bible then tells us how these renegades made common cause with the enemies of Israel, starting a great persecution of the Jewish people. By the same token it will be the renegades and the break-aways of our days, who will finally lay hands on the Catholics who are determined to remain faithful to their original loyalty and **Tradition**.

{All this goes to show that any break-away from Tradition, and the introduction of a new religion based on this fracture, has serious repercussions for the whole Church. All through history it has proven to be impossible for religious break-aways not to persecute the ones who refused to go with them, and who preferred to stay 'in their Father's house'. At present time it is unmistakable that from all over the world evidence can be gathered that Teilhardian nuns, brothers and priests are callous, and hard and cruel; that they are arrogant and indifferent: the very stuff that persecutors are made of ...}

5. Then the biblical parallel with our own days goes on:

"Then they fortified the City of David ... There they installed and army of sinful men, renegades, who fortified themselves inside it ... they were to prove a great trouble."

Before then it becomes too late to speak out 'because every outlet of episcopal departments has been occupied and fortified by modernists, proving to be a great trouble', I will write this article, now that it has been placed in context and perspective, in defense of my fellow Catholics, in defense of true Catholic Tradition, in defense of the Faith and Church I love, in defense of Truth, and finally, as an '*oratio pro domo*', in defense of myself.

Chapter One

A Fundamental Question
for the Catholics of Our Time

"A collective optimism, realistic and courageous, must definitely replace the pessimism and individualism, whose overgrown notions of **sin** and **salvation** have gradually burdened **and perverted** the Christian spirit ... Let us then acknowledge the situation honestly: not only the Imitation of Christ, **but also the Gospel itself needs to undergo this** (i.e. **his**) **correction**, and the whole world will make them undergo it. Why not say so?"

With these words, taken from his 1929 break with the Catholic Church: *The Human Sense*, Teilhard assumes before the Church of the 20th century, the same posture as Satan took up before Christ in the third recorded temptation: both assume to control the world. That Christ had to go through the full length of His Passion and Death in order to come to the end of the boast of Satan and to wrestle control from his grip, contains a dire message for the Church of our time, if it wants to be serious about outlasting the boast of Teilhard. In a subsequent chapter we will investigate if, maybe, this following of Christ 'in fine', 'till the bitter end' could hold the clue to the great Mystery of Vatican II.

There is no denying: Teilhard's thoughts and claims have made a shattering impact on the whole spectrum of human beliefs, so much so that, at least in the West, only great lovers of Our Lady seemed to have escaped the devastation of 'cyclone Teilhard'. Everywhere else, even in the seemingly most orthodox of circles, it is now assumed that **evolution** exists, and that it not only constitutes the matrix in which God 'created the world', but also forces itself upon us as the bridge, or the new synthesis, between Faith and faith, and between faith and science.

But is it?

All thought processes, all philosophies, and now even all theologies are supposed to meet on this bridge of evolution.

But do they?

This is one way of putting the most fundamental question of our time. Later on, we will have to reframe the <u>same</u> question as follows: 'Why is it that the part of the Church, which is most likely to follow Christ in His Passion and Death at the hand of their Heavenly Mother, also appears to be totally uncontaminated by the poison of evolution'?

In the *Phenomenon of Man* Teilhard elaborates on his boastful claims to the point of absurdity:

"Blind indeed are those who do not see the sweep of a movement whose orbit infinitely transcends the natural sciences and has successfully invaded the surrounding territory: chemistry, physics, sociology and even mathematics and the history of religions. One after another all the fields of human knowledge (theology!) have been shaken and carried away by the same under-water current in the direction of the study of a new development. Is evolution a theory, a system or hypothesis? It is much more: it is a general condition to which all theories, all hypotheses, all systems must bow, and which they must satisfy henceforth, if they are to be thinkable and true. Evolution is a curve that all lines must follow." (p. 241, Collins, Fontana paperback ed.)

So impressed are even non-Teilhardian theologians by this, that they are, if not seriously then at least hopefully, looking for the new synthesis in evolution. If only they had seriously studied what evolution has done to Teilhard … If, in *The Human Sense*, in order to give himself stature and authority to change the Catholic Church to his own vision, he boldly compares himself with **Buddha** and **Mohammed**, declaring that he is a world figure far more serious and revolutionary than they were, here, in this passage of *The Phenomenon of Man* he assumes the role of Satan in the third temptation of Christ, declaring himself to be greater than Christ; yes, even greater than God, for not only does Teilhard make God and Christ 'thinkable and true': he assigns to both the roles they are to play in evolution. Only the Divine Being, God, infinitely transcends natural sciences. But we just heard Teilhard declare that the mighty sweep of evolution does that. God, therefore, is subordinate to evolution, and **must** follow its curve in order to become thinkable and true.

And then Teilhard continues to show that only now there has emerged "the birth of an entirely new universe" through 'modern man's' awareness of evolution. And who made 'modern man' aware of this evolution that even ties down the Almighty? The 'modern man' Teilhard.

"What makes and classifies a modern man?" asks Teilhard. And his own answer to his own question in *The Phenomenon of Man* is absolutely classic:

"Having become capable of seeing in terms not of space and time alone, but also of **biological space-time**; <u>and above all</u>: having become incapable of seeing anything otherwise, anything, **not even himself** (Teilhard's stress)." (p. 241-242)

Since we are incapable of knowing anything else above and beyond evolution, and since evolution is essentially **biological**, Teilhard's god does not rise above biology. Is he serious about that? Oh yes.

"Is the kingdom of God a big family?" he asks in the epilogue to *The Phenomenon of Man*, and he answers his own question once again rather startlingly:

"Yes, in a sense it is. But in another sense it is a prodigious **biological operation**: that of the Redeeming Incarnation ..."

So what, according to Catholic Dogma, he should still be teaching, but refuses to teach: that Original Sin is passed on **through propagation**, that he now transfers to Redemption, making it a morphological, biological operation, as a function in his self-sufficient evolutionary system. What a boon for modern catechesis: "**redemption passed on through sex ...**". And this is precisely what Teilhard develops in his 1934 article: *The Sublimation of Chastity*, where the greatest height of "chastity" is achieved "in the use of a woman ..." (*The Evolution of Chastity*, Peking, Feb. 1934 in *Toward the Future*).

If more and more scientists are rejecting Darwinian and Marxist evolution, because it can no longer be adopted without sacrificing one's scientific integrity and intellectual honesty, and if this Teil-hardian nonsense cannot be accepted without loss of one's most treasured possession: the priceless gift of one's Catholic Faith and holy innocence, then **what evolution is left over** for Catholic academics to stir around in, in the hope of finding that elusive pearl of great wisdom, which will give the new synthesis they all crave?"

"**None**", has finally answered His Holiness Pope John Paul II with all the weight of the Catholic Magisterium behind him. For in this, the first systematic undertaking by a Pope to authentically trace the total absence of human evolution from Tradition to its origin and roots: the First Chapters in Genesis, the Holy Father not only asked the Catholic intelligentsia of today to stop looking in the wrong direction for a new synthesis in Catholic thought, he taught the whole Church a much more consoling truth. In telling us to stop looking altogether for an evolution that does not exist, he relieved us from the worry the accursed evolution of Teilhard de Chardin had placed on all of us, and he once again cleaned man, "the image of God", from the stain of all evolution. The consequences of this bold deed, once comprehended in all its significance, are grave. Had the Holy Father acted on the lead given by Card. Basil Hume, OSB, Primate of all England, and relieved Catholics and non-Catholics alike from believing in Marian dogmas as "only of secondary importance", the unholy jubilation of the Teilhardians and modernists would have been world-wide. But now that he has relieved the whole Church from faith in a non-existing evolution, thereby removing the modernists' idol Teilhard from its pedestal, he has probably signed his own death warrant …

I. The First Approach by the Holy Father, Dec 6, 1978

"The description of the creation of Man on the 6th day is some-what different from the preceding descriptions. In these descriptions we are witnesses only of the act of creation, expressed with the words: 'God said – Let there be ...'. Here, on the contrary, the author wishes to highlight first the intention and plan of the creator. We read in fact: 'Then God said, Let us make man in our image, after our likeness' (Genesis 1:26). As if the Creator entered into Himself ... as if, in a special way, He drew man from the mystery of His own Being. That is understandable, because it is not a question just of Being, but of the image. The image must 'reflect', it must, in a certain way, almost reproduce 'the substance' of its prototype. The Creator says, furthermore, "after our likeness". It is clear that it must not be understood as a portrait, but as a living being, who will live a life similar to that of God ...

It is clear to everyone, regardless of ideologies on the conception of the world, that man, though belonging to the visible world, to nature, is in some way differentiated from this nature itself ... He dominates it.

Science has made – and continues to make – a great many attempts in the various fields, to prove man's ties with the natural world and his dependence on it, in order <u>to integrate him into the history of the evolution</u> of various species. While respecting these researches, we cannot limit ourselves to them. If we analyse man in the depth of his being, we see that <u>he differs more from the world of nature then he resembles it</u> ... Let it be understood that the answer to the mystery of his humanity is **not** to be found along the path of similarity with the world of nature. **Man resembles God more than nature**."

II. The Second Approach by the Holy Father, Sep 12, 1979: Confirmation and Conclusion of this Sacred Teaching

"Man is created on earth together with the visible world. But at the same time the Creator orders him to subdue and have dominion over the earth: he is therefore placed over the world. Even though man is strictly bound to the visible world, nevertheless the biblical narrative does not speak of his likeness to the rest of creatures, but only to God. In the 7 day cycle of creation there is evident a precise graduated procedure. Man, however, is not created according to a natural succession, but the Creator seems to halt before calling him into existence, as if He were pondering within Himself to make a decision: 'let us make man in our image, after our likeness'.

The level of the first account of man's creation is particularly of a theological nature. An indication of that is especially the definition of man on the basis of his relationship with God ('in the image of God He created him'), which at the same time contains the affirmation **of the absolute impossibility of reducing man to the world**. Already in the light of the first phrases of the Bible, man cannot be either understood or explained completely in terms of categories taken from the 'world', that is, from the visible complex of bodies."

With this teaching, the Holy Father has blocked for ever the path to explain man through evolution. Formerly, the Catholic Church had already removed the creation of the human soul from evolution, stipulating that it is Church teaching that the human soul is directly created by God every time a human being is conceived. (Pope Pius XII in *Humani Generis*, 1950, and Pope John XXIII in *Mater Et Magister*, 1961). But, while leaving the question of evolution of the human body an open question, Pope Pius XII stipulated two requirements:

> (i) Evolution of the body may **not** be taught as an established fact, and

> (ii) "there **must** be a readiness on all sides to accept the arbitrament of the Church as being entrusted by Christ with the right to interpret Scripture, and the duties to safe guard the Doctrine of the Faith. (*Humani Generis*, 1950. And also stated in an *Allocution to Scientists*, Nov 30, 1941.)

And now, from his successor, Pope John Paul II, we have received this solemn teaching. The human **body** has now also been removed from any evolutionary system (if such a system should exist), and what is more, the Holy Father is teaching this doctrine as contained in Genesis. In other words: he is using his supreme authority as teacher of the Church to explain Scripture, telling us how Sacred Scripture – in this case the first chapters of Genesis – is to be understood and explained. And now that this has come to pass, we must obey the injunction given to us by Pope Pius XII, and by giving heed to this teaching, 'show the readiness to accept the arbitrarement of the Church' when she uses Her God given right 'to interpret Scripture'.

In conclusion of this first chapter on **Tradition**, I like to point out two things:

1. Catholics must now look elsewhere for their inspiration to discover 'this elusive new synthesis'. The path of evolution has now been effectively blocked for them. As I will develop further on in this article: I am by no means convinced that we are in need of 'a new synthesis'. Maybe, in Vatican II, the Catholic Church has brought out something old from the great treasure and storehouse of the Deposit of Faith, that we had forgotten, and which, once brought to light again, may be recognised as this new synthesis.

2. If the Magisterium of the Church has now repeatedly and formally removed the creation of the body and of the soul of human beings from any system of evolution, then 'evolution' of the plants and animals has now become a dead letter, emptied out of all meaning, since the enemies of the Church only wanted evolution accepted in so far as it degraded man, 'created in the image and likeness of God', and especially would degrade the **God-Man** Jesus Christ, and His Immaculately Conceived Mother.

Maybe one day, this evolution too, will be excluded from Catholic thinking by the Book of Genesis, where, in the <u>order</u> of Creation it is stated, that God created the plants on the <u>third</u> day and the sun on the <u>fourth</u> day. If these 'biblical days' are periods of millions of years, and if the biblical order is correct, then the plants must have lived for millions of years without the light of the sun. We know that the order of Creation is inerrant ...

Chapter Two

"I am the Lord Your God" (Ex. 20:1, Deut. 5:6)

With these words of the Old Testament, echoing the words of God spoken to Abraham (Gen. 17:1), we will start a proper investigation into the deep roots of Catholic Tradition, uprooted on such a distressingly vast scale by the onslaught of Teilhardian evolution. For it cannot be denied that, after Vatican II, many fair-minded Catholics had been puzzled by the fact that to them, in spite of what they were made to believe the Sacred Tradition of the Catholic Church had always appeared free from the taint of evolution. The first chapter of this essay has conclusively shown them that they can now set their minds at rest in the firm conviction, that their original beliefs and intuition were right, now that the highest teaching authority in the Church has declared, from authentic interpretation of Scripture, that this sacred Tradition does **not** contain human evolution.

However, the Catholic certainty that Tradition is non-evolutionary, does not make it immediately clear what it then is, and so we have not yet been relieved from the obligation to explore what Tradition is in the Mind of the Church.

In a sincere search for the Truth about Tradition, we may, as a first approximation, let ourselves be guided by what the Catholic Church actually rejected in disowning evolution.

Extreme evolution, in total opposition to Creation, accepts **chance** as its first principle of the origin of everything, together with the assumption (in order to be 'logical') of the **eternity of**

matter and – of course – **only matter**. Furthermore, it assumes that the **mechanics** of evolution (1) allow it to go from the simple to the complex, contrary to fundamental laws of Physics, notably the Second Law of Thermodynamics, which states that every running-down system loses energy, not gains it; and (2) allow 'mutations' combined with 'natural selection' to cause the differentiation in the innumerable species of animals and plants. In spite of the fact that all we know, and have positive evidence of, is that mutations of genes have only caused misery; and always within the same species, i.e. within the same genetic code.

Having rejected **chance** as the root-cause of the wonderful order in Nature, the **eternity of matter**, and also **matter: the only reality**, as incompatible with Revealed Truth (and so incompatible with human intelligence also, since there is no clash between Revealed Truth and any other truth the human mind is capable of ascertaining), the Church did not have to intrude into the specific scientific areas mentioned above, to denounce evolution as a rival for Creation.

1. Vital to Teilhard was his intellectual starting point: his principle of **identity**, what to us is a logical absurdity. Evolution, as we know, clashes violently with the 'real distinction' principle in true philosophy, which was succinctly expressed by the late Pope John XXIII in his first encyclical: *Ad Petri Cathedram* as follows: "Contrary 'truths' cannot exist". A truth, e.g. "God exists", and its contrary: "God does not exist", cannot be both true in the same sense. By adopting his 'principle of identity' for the sake of his pre-

cious 'evolution', Teilhard veered sharply away from sound logic and true philosophy. The principle of **identity** denies the '**Principle of Contradiction**' by which contrary truths cannot exist, so that contrary truths **can** exist side by side to avoid contradiction. Of course, Teilhard never clearly announced his new principle of identity. It had to be culled from his writings, but he clearly assumed it in all his contradictions which were always covered in a jargon of claptrap masquerading for pseudo-scientific nonsense. I have dealt extensively with this fundamental question of Teilhardian evolution in my first article in this whole series: *Teilhard De Chardin and the Dutch Catechism.*

What are some of the consequences of the adoption of this principle of **sameness**, or **identity**.

(i) The Creator becomes indistinguishable from His creation in one evolving mass. The supernatural and natural become fused into one level: evolution. Not only did God cease to become distinct from evolution: human beings too lost their identity and individuality in Teilhard's system, to become 'monads' or building blocks, totally subordinate to the 'whole'. No wonder Teilhard favoured totalitarian systems, collectivism and the white supremacy, since a white man: himself, had discovered evolution, and had given it 'direction'.

(ii) The principle of **sameness** destroys <u>absolutes</u>. It makes absolute Truth, an absolute moral order, an Absolute Existence, God, impossible and inoperative. Everything is subordinate to the one absolute he accepts: the evolving material universe "to which all systems must bow, if they want to be thinkable and true".

(iii) Since in evolution, everything is more or less the same (all evolving towards omega-point), all religions are essentially the same. So any missionary bitten by this bug becomes a social worker mainly for material development, since such an attitude stifles all desire to make converts. This explains the moratorium on missionary activity adopted by the World Council of Churches' *World Conference on Missions* in Bangkok in 1973, as described so eloquently by Prof. Peter Beyerhaus in his incredible book *Bangkok '73*. In 1961, the WCC in another World Conference, had officially adopted the 'Christology of Teilhard' when it made the 'cosmic Christ' its own. So there it is: cause and effect.

(iv) One other result of the adoption of the principle of sameness in an evolutionary system is that the creation is the **same** as re-arranging pre-existing matter. Teilhard absolutely denies God the power to create *ex-nihilo*, from nothing. Being part of the evolving mass, He can only rearrange and unite **through us** pre-existing matter. To create = to unite. (Teilhard).

2. A second aspect which **by necessity** is irrevocably attached to Teilhardian evolution is that this evolution **inevitably** ends up in omega point (Teilhard's god). Now, if this god is being mistakenly claimed by millions of his followers as OUR GOD, then it becomes obvious that Teilhard is asking those millions of followers 'to let go of the cross, and take his armchair ride to God'. And this has become the most fascinating call in Teilhardian evolution: it is being portrayed as inevitably ending up in God, since God is supposed to be part of this evolving process ... Read again what I quoted above from his essay *The Human Sense*, how he heaps scorn on people who still believe in the primacy of the Fall, in expiation and the scorn of temporal things: they are falsifying themselves ... There is no need for ...

Frightful indeed are the consequences of this 'fascination'. Here are only some of them:

(i) The destruction of authority. If everybody's path in evolution ends up in God then there is no need for anybody to tell me how to secure my own salvation. This is the foundation of the revolt against *Humanae Vitae*, and the foundation of the slogan: 'the Pope can stay out of my bedroom'. Teilhard supports all rebellion.

(ii) Coupled with that is of course the total and absolute 'freedom of conscience' claimed by these people. Teilhardian freedom of conscience absolves people from the grave obligation of forming one's conscience on the Truth. There is only one absolute truth for Teilhardians: they end up inevitably in god, no matter what they do ... (Catholics recognise this as a '**sin against the Holy Spirit**, a **sin against the Light**, which is the reason why it is almost impossible to convert Teilhardian Catholics. This is the foundation of the 'church of darkness', the church without the Light, as foreseen by Pope St. Pius X; and this finally is the foundation of the great persecutions foretold by Our Lady of Fatima: Teilhardian Catholics will rather murder and persecute than give up this 'new religion'.)

(iii) This 'armchair ride to god' aspect of evolution destroys the meaning of suffering, the meaning of the Cross and of expiation of sin. This aspect of Teilhardian aberrations, therefore, directly supports abortion and euthanasia.

3. To people who kept untrammelled their Supernatural, Infused, Divine Gift of Catholic Faith in spite of the relentless propaganda 'to let go of the Cross and join the multitudes in this armchair ride to god', the foregoing is so obviously anti-Catholic, that not even with the wildest stretch of the

imagination could it be called, let alone adopted as, 'the new Catholicism'. Yet, this is what it is all about. This is the new craze of all the theologians before which bishops have fallen silent and hesitant, afraid of being singled out as out of step with Vatican II, modern thought and the rediscovery of 'Christianity'.

But where is the 'Catholic' flag that would cover this rotten cargo, and would pass it on without close scrutiny as the new Catholicism? If we can discover that we will have come face to face with Satan in his most devastating travesty as an 'angel of light' (2 Cor. 11:14) in our times.

The bait held out to tired Catholics, delectable to the proud human mind of modern man, but impregnated with the deadly poison of Teilhardian evolution, was contained in what Teilhard himself considered his most important work, written in 1926, and for which he unsuccessfully tried to obtain an Ecclesiastical Imprimatur to his dying days: *Le Milieu Divin.*

In this work Teilhard develops the view of the extension of Christ in space and time, a most laudable and Catholic beginning. The dominion of Christ, the Kingship of Christ are truly Christian ideas. But Teilhard, dissatisfied, because of his evolution, with seeing the Catholic Church pointed out as the Mystical Body of Christ, continuing His Supernatural work of redeeming from sin by methods He Himself had adopted, now started to point to 'the Universe' as the true extension of Christ. For this he had to coin a new word: 'cosmic Christ'. The material universe-in-evolution is to the 'cosmic Christ' what the Sacred Humanity was to the historic Christ. The job of this new 'mistical body of the cosmic Christ' is now to help Christ redeem evolution until the glorious ending in the revelation of omega point. The two immediate consequences of this fatal switch from the Catholic Church to the material universe as the extension of Christ is space and time, with the consequent switch in role of the Redemption, are:

(i) the abolition of sin: original sin and individual sin. Teilhard, in many places, will only admit 'mistakes' in the proper implementation of the work of evolution. Christ, in his sacred humanity, could not sin (a truly Catholic thought). We, in the material universe-in-evolution also cannot sin, since we are the sacred humanity of the cosmic Christ (a truly satanic concept). According to Teilhard: this is what the Redemption of Christ was all about. We may now start to understand the world-wide acceptance of Teilhardian evolution, if we see the world-wide acceptance of the abolition of sin and the drop in Catholic confessions.

(ii) the acceptance of redemption as being primarily a **biological** function in the material universe. I refer the reader to the Teilhardian quotes printed above. If sex propagates the new extension of Christ in biological space-time, and advancing this extension is

synonymous with extending 'redemption', then truly, according to Teilhard, redemption is propagated
by sex, any sex. Now, what teenager, or any human
being tired of the old morality, would not like to
have this explained to him or her in the new catechesis rampant today because of the timidity of the
bishops? Teilhard and the infamous *Dutch Catechism* are directly responsible for the removal of
guilt from the sexual aberrations and eroticism
prevalent today. No wonder people addicted to this
are reluctant to give up Teilhardism and its evolution which pretend to give a 'Catholic' basis to the
most perverse sexual aberrations.

If this is becoming widely accepted as the new interpretations
of Catholic Tradition, then – I repeat – good Catholics will be mar-
tyred for refusing to accept this Satan-in-Catholic-garb …

So let us proceed to remove the 'Catholic flag' and let us hold
up this rotten cargo against the brilliant Light of **True Catholic
Tradition** from way back: its **Old Testament Roots**. If the teachings of Teilhard cannot be traced back to Abraham and Moses,
then they are **not** found in the Old Testament Revelation, and consequently are not passed on into the Revelation of the New Testament. For **Tradition** means '**Traditio Revelationis**': the passing on
of Revelation from one generation to the next. No true teaching
can ever be slipped in somewhere along the line entirely from the
outside. The true development of Dogma has its roots in Revelation.

(For the benefit of the reader, I will repeat the numbering as started above, going through the same sequence as started there.)

(1) The principle of identity and sameness.

Since this is obviously the foundation of **Pantheism**, no trace of this principle is anywhere in Jewish or Christian literature. Logically, this principle is untenable, and the principle of contradiction, whereby a truth and its contrary cannot be both true in the same sense at the same time, remains the foundation of human logic. Teilhard invented this 'principle' to do away with contradictions and the 'real distinction' principle underlying Thomism and all human thought. Like evolution, it was adopted by sinful human beings to explain away God and the distinction between good and evil, obviously for ulterior motives.

(i)   This principle, if adopted, allows the Creator to become indistinguishable from His creation. This is so patently in contradiction of the Old Testament and the whole practice of the Jewish religion, that it could never find its way into the New Testament Revelation of God in Jesus Christ. Teilhard admits that only he himself discovered evolution, so Christ in His life time really did not think of it, and it was only through Teilhard that the 'cosmic Christ' became aware of evolution. But even so: once 'discovered', it must be possible to **see** it now traced clearly back to an Old Testament origin, and a New Testament fulfillment. This is patently impossible.

The words 'I Am The Lord Your God', quoted at the heading of this chapter, and 'In the Beginning God (already in existence) created (from nothing) heaven and earth' (not in existence from all eternity and so distinct from God who pre-existed His creation) show clearly the real distinction between God and His creation, destroying the principle of sameness. So, the Hypostatic Union between the Second Person of the Blessed Trinity and His Sacred Humanity cannot be explained by means of **identity**, since this principle was **not** passed on from the Jewish Tradition into the Christian one.

(ii) The destruction of absolutes by the principle of identity.

Here we meet, once again, the 'heresy' of **Nominalism**, from which, according to Prof. Richard Weaver in his brilliant book *Ideas Have Consequences*, Western Civilisation has suffered with a gradually increasing intensity, until it produced its final and most poisonous offspring: evolution. Obviously, Teilhard and his innumerable followers are only fooling themselves with words, **names** (**Nomen** in Latin), denying any reality behind those **names**. Thus they can be arranged in any order or sequence without contradiction, as long as the underlying message comes out sharply: 'There is no God: you are free to do as you please ...' That is all the various nominalists down the centuries ever had in common. The Jewish Tradition accepted the Universal Validity of the Ten Commandments, the Universal Truth of the existence of God, not dependant on human consent and not changing with the various stages in their history. They knew how to return to God in repentance, showing a deep awareness of religious submission: not only to the Will of God, but also to the acceptance in Truth of the existence of a **never varying Law** coming from an unchanging God. This deep awareness of absolutes found its way into the New Covenant and so into the Deposit of Faith entrusted to the Catholic Church.

(iii)   The acceptance that 'all religions are the same' by the principle of identity.

This too is not borne out by the Jewish Tradition in the Old Regime. All through Scripture, the Jews have expressed their gladness to be Yahweh's people; have expressed deep awareness 'that God had not dealt with other people like He had done with them', and have shown in their repeated 'conversions' and returns to God that they were sinning if they followed other religions. God revealed that He considered the relationship He had with Israel as that of the Bridegroom with His Bride, and that this relationship required faithfulness on both sides; and that unfaithfulness on the part of Israel, i.e. following other 'gods' in other religions, constituted a lapse into the state of a whore. Since this was a true revelation by God, it too found its way into the New Testament as the foundation of all the missionary activity of the Catholic Church.

(iv)   Through the adoption of the principle of identity, our human activity of uniting is identical to 'helping' God create; and God's Act of creation is really only nothing but helping us unite pre-existing matter.

The idea (and even more so the reality) of a creation out of nothing is repugnant to evolution since it postulates, of necessity, a Creator totally independent from His creation. It is Catholic Dogma that **matter** became existent **in time**, and not 'from eternity' co-existent with God. There is not a trace of the latter to be found in Jewish writings and practices in the Old Covenant, and so this non-existence of a belief in the eternity of matter, co-existent with God, was carried over into the New Order, where the true belief in creation became perpetuated.

2.   The **Inevitability** of salvation.

This idea is so repugnant to the true followers of Christ, that it constitutes sheer blasphemy. The idea of telling everybody to hop onto the jolly bandwagon of the world, do what you like, believe what you like, and evolution will see to it that you end up in omega-god, is so repulsive as to be wholly satanic. It is obvious that evolution was invented to allow for the unlimited licentiousness we see all around us. The mark of the 'church of darkness': '**No curb on the passions**' as foreseen and foretold by Pope St. Pius X, finds its realisation in this aspect of Teilhardian evolution, the true manifestation of this church of darkness.

All I can say here, in relation to the Jewish situation, is, that it was the **false tradition** of the Scribes and Pharisees which equated 'being children of Abraham' with 'being saved' that caused the death of Christ ...

And so we can be brief with (i) destruction of authority, (ii) the absolute freedom of conscience and (iii) the destruction of the meaning of suffering, which follow immediately from the adoption of the principle of the inevitability of salvation. There always was authority in the Jewish Tradition; Christ 'taught with authority' and left absolute authority vested in His Vicar on earth. Absolute freedom of conscience is self-destructive. The mystery of suffering was not regarded in the Old Testament as meaningless, even if not fully understood. What was understood, through the Messianic prophecies of the 'Servant of God', was that suffering became closely associated with expiation, the meaning which was taken up and fully developed in the New Testament by the Sacred Passion and Death of the Son of God on the Cross. This meaning was put before us once again in all its eternal significance and ramifications by Our Lady at Fatima, when She asked all of us **to bring sacrifices for poor sinners**.

3. The question of the universe being the true extension of Christ in time and space (or more precisely: **biological** space-time according to Teilhard).

    As stated and claimed by Teilhard the whole idea is preposterous, as can be seen from the Church's refusal to give an Imprimatur to the book in which these fundamental misconceptions were presented as a viable alternative interpretation of traditional teaching.

The universe is matter, passive existence. Matter only becomes 'alive' if animated by a soul as its life-giving principle. Christ is only concerned with beings which have an immortal soul, really distinct from their bodies, <u>human</u> beings. For the universe to be an extension of Christ, it must have a soul, the soul of Christ: the same one that animated His Sacred Humanity on earth. We know by Divine Revelation that this Sacred Soul reunited with His Body in the grave at the time of the Resurrection, and that it **did not unite** with anything else. We further know (i) that human beings become incorporated in Christ's Divine Life through Baptism, and (ii) that Christ, through His Holy Spirit works in souls towards this incorporation if not yet obtained. The material universe does not come into this, least of all in the role assigned to it by Teilhard: of taking over the redemption to the point of inevitability. The **duality** between God and man, man endowed with free will to choose between Good and Evil, and endowed with an intellect to guide his free will, is Old Testament Tradition incorporated in the New Testament in no uncertain terms.

> (i) The inevitability of evolution to end up in god-omega has abolished sin.
>
> Since this evolution does not exist, its diabolical offspring: the inevitability of salvation also does not exist. According to good advice from St. Paul, 'we

must work out our salvation in fear and trembling'. (Phil. 2:12). The whole concept of 'abolition of sin because of a <u>material</u> direction of the universe: evolving to omega-point' is making a caricature of the Love by which Christ came to redeem us, which of course is precisely the idea of Satan behind this whole falsification.

(ii) Unbridled sex is the cosmic Christ: the **biological** space-time extension of the kingdom of god.

The mind really boggles and reels when we come to realise what exactly Teilhardism is, and how it came about that all the great names in theology have advocated it as the new fascinating insights into post-Vatican II Catholicism. We can only pray and bring sacrifices for the millions of souls who have been seduced by this teaching in Catholic schools. All we can say here is that Teilhard himself practised what he preached:

"Every day the glaring evidence is that no man can do without a woman, as he cannot do without light, oxygen and vitamins. From this critical moment (i.e. when he first fell in love …) nothing has developed in me but under the glance and influence of a woman" quotes *The Rock* (Ceylon, vol. 2, Feb 1974) as the very words of Teilhard de Chardin; and then the paper continues with a list of Teilhard's lovers under the heading:

"Teilhard's Uninterrupted Succession of Sweethearts".

Corruptio optimi pessima: the corruption of the best becomes the very worst …

There, but for the Grace of God, go I …

Chapter Three

The Virgin Was Not Deceived

In the previous chapters we showed clearly from internal criticism, as well as from external comparisons with Catholic Tradition, why the Catholic Church has resolutely and steadfastly refused to accept Teilhardism as a new and exciting interpretation of Catholicism, in spite of the rebellion sustained by millions of his followers.

Why would that be so? How could the Church tell, especially in the early stages when things were not brought into the open as they are now?

Furthermore, to many devout Catholics, the previous exercise in this article could quite well have been totally unnecessary as far as their own inner convictions are concerned, even if such an expose will greatly help them to bring others, less fortunate than themselves, to a true change of heart.

Again we ask ourselves: Why would that be? How did those simple Catholics know the difference? How did they remain unaffected?

The answer to all these questions is the same. When all is said and done, the true Catholic Church, in and through Her clear-sighted children, remained very close to **Our Lady**.

From the foregoing it has been made abundantly clear that Teilhardism is the total and absolute antithesis of Our Lady.

St. Louis Grignion de Montfort has stated in his magnificent treatise on the True Devotion, that God has created only **one enmity**, but it is an irreconcilable one, which will increase in strength and bitterness even to the end of time. This is the enmity between Mary, His sublime Mother, and the Devil; between the children and servants of the Blessed Virgin, and the children and instruments of Satan. The most terrible of enemies whom God has raised up against Satan is Mary, His Blessed Mother.

Well, if there is **only one enmity**, and Teilhardism is the total and absolute opposite to **Our Blessed Lady**, then Teilhardism belongs in the camp of the Devil, from whom it got its inspiration and drive. It is as simple as that. And the inspiration and drive to reject it and to undo its damage must then come from God and His Holy Mother.

Since this is an essay on Catholic Tradition, we will part company with Teilhard's infernal system; and for the sake of the millions seduced by it we will concentrate our attention on the deep spiritual roots of Marian piety in Catholic Tradition.

For this we can do no more than highlight the solid foundations of Marian Devotion laid down by the Apostles and the earliest Christian writers under the direct inspiration of the Holy Spirit, on which foundation all subsequent generations of Christians have built the rich, spiritual cathedral of veneration and love directed towards the Mother of God.

1. The Virgin Was Not Deceived

The earliest outpourings of love and gratitude for Mary, the Mother of Jesus, did not spring so much from an understanding of Her extraordinary privileges, as from a deep supernatural grasp of what She had **done**. And, according to the exceptionally beautiful teaching of Vatican II, that is still the foundation of Marian devotion today. For Vatican II went right back to the roots of Marian piety in the 1st Century of Christianity: to the profound grasp the Apostles had on the intimate connection between the Fall and the Redemption. Between the Revealed Order of the Fall and Original Sin, and the order-in-reverse the Redemption from that sin took, and the restoration to the state of Adopted Children of God.

And in gracing Our Lady with the title of 'the New Eve', the early Christians (and Vatican II) not only showed that they fully understood, in the Light of the Holy Spirit, what it must have cost Mary to produce the Redeemer and to cooperate with Him all the way to Calvary; they not only showed their own profound gratitude and love for what She had done and suffered to produce the Church, His Body; but in laying this foundation they made it impossible for all future generations to forget the earliest inspiration, no matter how wonderful the 'cathedral' would become as the insights into Her mystery would grow and deepen.

In revealing the role of Christ as the New Adam, St. Paul did not only hint at Mary's role of the New Eve, since it was impossible for those early Christians not to point to a deep spiritual meaning of a New Eve, in pointing out a New Adam; but he actually paid the greatest honour to Our Lady in the pages of the New Testament outside the Gospels. And it is precisely this revelation by St. Paul from God, which has remained the **intuition**, (one could almost call it the Catholic instinct) of Marian love and devotion for all future generations.

In 1 Tim. 2:14, St. Paul makes a profound observation which has a direct bearing on this question. Here he says:

"Adam was not deceived, but the woman was deceived, and so became a transgressor …"

We know that St. Paul had an accurate grasp of the profound doctrine of the order-in-reverse by which salvation came into the world. Here he shows that he knew the difference between the Sin of Eve, and Adam's Sin which became the Original Sin. By showing that he knew that the first Woman was deceived by listening to the Fallen Angel, St. Paul also shows that he fully understood **that Mary was not deceived** by listening to the message of an Archangel that came to Her from God. After Eve's sin, Adam's hands were tied. Before Mary's **fiat**, God's Hands were tied, so to speak. God fully depended on Mary's free consent. And for a second time, for one moment, the fate of the whole human race was in the hands of a woman: 'Would She believe the Angel, or not …?' She obeyed … Therein lies all the greatness of Womanhood. And when the impact of this Revelation started to become understood by the early Church, there was no longer any holding back: '**The Virgin was not deceived** …'. From that moment on the Catholic Church **bound Herself to the Virgin**, so that, in time and eternity, She Herself would also never be deceived. And could continue to 'untie God's Hands' and become – like Mary – a cause of salvation for Herself and for the whole human race.

Here, then, is the explanation of the answer I gave previously: why it is that Catholics, who had 'bound themselves to the Virgin' by a great personal love and devotion, managed to remain unaffected by the Teilhardian deception spread right across the world. 'The Virgin was not deceived …'. And so, the very first grace She will obtain for Her devoted children is also 'not to be deceived'; or not to remain for long in a state of deception or confusion, if fallen into it. The opposite is equally true: going away from Her, or from obedience to the only Church of which She is the proto-type, is taking the first steps towards **deception**, of which the history of Christianity – tragically enough – contains innumerable examples …

2. Mary Undoing the 'Knot of Eve'

Not satisfied by revealing to us the deep spiritual roots of Marian devotion and love within the Catholic Church, roots that go beyond Her glorious pre-selection and privileges, to Her active and painful cooperation as the New Eve with the New Adam, the early Church and Vatican II now proceed to divulge the extent of Mary's participation in the work of the redemption of the fallen human race.

"The knot of Eve's disobedience (Remember, it tied the hands of her husband!) was untied by Mary's obedience. What the virgin Eve bound through her unbelief, Mary loosened by Her Faith." (*Lumen Gentium*, 56; quoting St. Irenaeus.)

"In no other way can that which is tied be untied, unless the very windings of the knot are gone through in reverse. Thus then the knot of the disobedience of Eve was untied through the obedience of Mary." (St. Irenaeus.)

The knot of Eve was finally untied on Calvary. This can only mean that, if Our Lady undid Eve's knot, as the early Church and the Council teach us here, then She went through every twist and turn and winding Her Divine Son had to go through to undo the tangle of Sin, right up to Calvary. The Vatican Council is quite specific that this is the meaning that we must give to Mary's altogether singular participation (*Lumen Gentium*, 61) in, and cooperation with, the work of Redemption:

"This union of the Mother with the Son in the work of salvation was manifested from the time of Christ's virginal conception up to His death." (*Lumen Gentium*, 57.)

Every minute, every hour, every day ...

"Thus the Blessed Virgin advanced in Her pilgrimage of Faith and loyally endured Her union with Her Son unto the Cross." (*Lumen Gentium*, 58.)

At the Annunciation She had willingly said **fiat**, let it be done. Now, after a lifetime of practice, She would not take it back. She would live out the last dread implications of those words.

And in the deep appreciation of the Mystery involved, the Second Vatican Council went still further, and showed us why this union between the New Adam and the New Eve cannot be broken, by teaching us exactly where this union lies:

"In an altogether singular way She cooperated **by Her Obedience, Faith, Hope and burning Love** in the Saviour's work of restoring Supernatural life to souls ..." (*Lumen Gentium*, 61.)

It does not lie in Mary's preselection. It does not lie in Her prerogatives and privileges: it lies beyond the reach of any power in Heaven or on earth, on a level where a creature unites itself to the Infinite for better or for worse, in the single determination of mind and will in Faith, Hope, Obedience and burning Love …

3. Mary, Typos of the Church.

And the Sacred Council is aware that only there, in the rarified atmosphere of absolute holiness, in such a presence of, and union with, the Infinite Holiness of God, does the Blessed Virgin become the model and Proto-type of only one Church on earth: the One, Holy, Catholic and Apostolic Church, regardless of the sinfulness of Catholics. For the mystery of the Catholic Church is such that, although composed of sinful children of Eve, She Herself is nevertheless also beyond the reach of sin. 'The spotless Bride of the Lamb of God', 'without stain or wrinkle'.

"In the Blessed Virgin, the Church has already reached that perfection in which She is 'without spot or wrinkle' (Eph. 5:27). But the faithful are still struggling to grow in holiness by overcoming sin. And so they lift up their eyes to Mary, who shines forth to the whole community of the elect as the model of virtues. The Church, devoutly meditating on Her, and contemplating Her in the Light of the Word-made-Man, reverently enters more deeply into the Supreme Mystery of the Incarnation, and is made more and more conformed to Her Spouse. Having entered deeply into the history of Salvation, Mary … prompts the faithful to come to Her Son, to His Sacrifice (the Mass) and to love of the Father. Seeking after the glory of Christ, **the Church becomes more like Her lofty Type**, constantly advancing in Faith, Hope and Love, and seeking and carrying out the Divine Will in all things." (*Lumen Gentium*, 65.)

"The Church indeed contemplating Her hidden sanctity, imitating Her charity, and faithfully carrying out the Will of the Father, likewise becomes a **mother** by receiving the word of God in Faith. For She too is a **Virgin** who keeps in its entirety and purity the Faith She pledged Her Spouse. Imitating the Mother of the Lord, and by the power of the Holy Spirit, she keeps intact Faith, firm Hope and sincere Love." (*Lumen Gentium*, 64.)

This will have to do to bring out how deeply Marian is Catholic Tradition, and how the Church depends on this Sacred Tradition to see Her safely through the most terrible time of Her existence: the reign of AntiChrist.

I refer my readers to *Lumen Gentium* 63, where they can read how the Second Vatican Council bases its teaching on Mary, Typos of the Church, on the insights of St. Ambrose, a Father of the Church; who, through his reputation for holiness and learning, was instrumental in receiving St. Augustine into the Church.

To conclude this chapter on one of the most beloved topics on which one can write and meditate, I will recapitulate it for you in a convenient prayer form.

(i) When we begin by saying: "The Angel of the Lord declared unto Mary, and She conceived by the Holy Spirit", and all during the subsequent Hail Mary … we can honour Our Blessed Lady for not having been deceived when She accepted the Angel's message in such great Faith, and we can ask Her to keep us close to Her for the next 6 hours, so that we too may not be deceived during that time.

(ii) When we say: "Behold the Handmaid of the Lord ..." we can honour Our Lady by remembering how much She has done and suffered to undo for us the 'knot of Eve'. And we can ask Her during the subsequent Hail Mary to help us undo the 'knot of Eve' of our time and in our own environment for the next 6 hours, out of gratitude to Her and Jesus, for the love of souls.

(iii) When we say: "And the Word was made flesh ..." we can honour Our Blessed Mother by remembering how Her fiat became, through the Incarnation, a cause of salvation for all mankind, and we can ask Her that we may imitate that too for the next 6 hours, and that we too may be in our small way a true 'model of the Church' for all we come in contact with.

(iv) Finally, when we say: "Pray for us, O Holy Mother of God ...", we can honour Our Lady for the power She received from God in return for Her faithful service given to Him. And we can implore Her to keep us under Her powerful protection for the next 6 hours, **and to even let us have a share in that power** in our struggle with the 'powers of darkness' to undo 'the knot of Eve' for Her.

Six hours is thus all we have to worry about, and then we look forward to meeting and honouring Her again in the next 6 hours. Filling our day in this way with the Marian influence, we not only faithfully obey the Church's wishes; we not only please and honour God through Mary; we not only become more Christ-like through Mary: we are, at the same time, in deep spiritual touch with each other and with generations of Catholic Tradition which, before us, have changed the face of the earth … through Mary, and with Her.

Chapter Four

The Bride of the Lamb of God

Here I will take my time developing what I see as the great Mystery of the Second Vatican Council, and how this great Council shares in the Mystery of the Church. First I will give a brief outline of my central position, then, starting from the periphery and some pertinent questions, I will slowly advance to the centre; where, once again, I will place the Mystique of our times in the mainstream of Catholic Tradition as requested by the title of this article.

A Preliminary Outline

(i) I am absolutely convinced that in spite of the warnings and condemnations of the great Pope St. Pius X, a **School** of Modernism in his days, has been developed into the **System** of Modernism of Teilhard de Chardin's evolution.

(ii) I am equally convinced that a totally erroneous philosophy has been introduced into Catholic thinking, and has been accepted there; that this philosophy is the cornerstone of the Teilhardian system; that this philosophy so-called has been foreseen and condemned by Pope Pius XII in *Humani Generis*, before it burst onto the world scene. What this great Pope feared might happen, we see now being erected on a grand scale: this philosophy is being used to underpin

Catholic doctrine, Catholic theology, Catholic catechesis; and is relentlessly being used to be the basis for the erroneous interpretations of Vatican II. But if this philosophy is <u>in error</u>, then errors in Catholic philosophy, theology, catechesis and Vatican II interpretations are now being portrayed as authentic Catholic teaching, fulfilling to the letter the grave words of Pope St. Pius X (*Pascendi*):

"... so that there is no part of Catholic truth which they leave untouched, none that they do not strive to corrupt".

(iii) I am equally convinced that this false philosophy of **Sameness** and **Identity** has been introduced by Teilhard into Jesuitism, and I was personally there when in the early 1940's the Jesuits introduced this erroneous philosophy **as the new Thomism**: first into Catholic tertiary levels; but gradually spread out over all levels, mainly through the infamous **Dutch Catechism**, which they wrote.

(iv) Finally, I am convinced that at present time (as in the 16th Century) a (Teilhardian) church of darkness and disobedience is in the process of separating itself from the Catholic Church; and that, before long, this will end up in global persecutions of the Catholic Church. For, just as the First Fall and the First Original Sin, evoked from God the response of the Incarnation and Sacred Passion and Death of His Son, so this 'second original sin' of the great and universal apostasy necessitates the passion and 'almost death' (Pope Benedict XV) of the Catholic Church, **because of the**

parallelism in St. Paul's theology, by which the Catholic Church is the Bride of Christ, held up by St. Paul as an example to any Christian Bride: to follow her man wherever he may go.

(v) The cornerstone of my convictions is the uniqueness of **Fatima**, and its long preparation of devout souls before the final onslaught. If, because of its uniqueness, it spans the centuries: touching on the First Prophecy in Paradise right to its fulfillment, then this fulfillment must be of **global dimension**. Now it is obvious that in contemporary history we are dealing with the formation of a 'one-world church' (foretold by Pope St. Pius X) and with 'one-world government'. If such a world-wide agglomerate succeeds in forcing itself on humanity, we do not need much imagination to establish that it will be inimical to human freedom, and to a Catholic Church. This means persecutions, a visible demise of the Catholic Church, **but nevertheless an uninterrupted Tradition of the Catholic Church to the next generation** by the very people who have shown the greatest '*sensus Catholicus*', Catholic sense, in having stayed very close to Our Lady, Our Lady of Fatima.

This touches directly on what I maintain is the central message and meaning of Vatican II: <u>Martyrdom</u>. In page after page Vatican II does **not** tell us how to **identify** ourselves with the world as the rampant false philosophy of Teilhard tries to tell us; but how to surrender ourselves to the world in martyrdom, out of great compassion for a sin-

ful humanity. There is a hair-line of difference, but it is absolute, and therefore eternal. The same difference between
saying: that the Incarnation shows God's love for the world
to the point of **identification** (Teilhardism), and the true
Catholic teaching that it shows God's love for us to the
point of surrender and immolation for sin. In page after
page Vatican II teaches us how to take the world and our
separated brethren into account in our effective daily immolation for their sake. The outgoing and outpouring of
our Catholic spirit is **not** to the embrace of the world in a
Teilhardian sense, but in a crucified sense. It is the final
fruit of nineteen centuries of teaching and practice, like the
final day was in the life of Christ after three years of teaching. Vatican II is **not** a new beginning after so many centuries of false starts (Teilhardian interpretation), but a crown
and glory, even if for a while, the crown is made of thorns
…

A Few Peripheral Questions

(i) Isn't this drawing too much on pre-Vatican II sources, ob-
scuring an authentic contribution made by this Council?

Pre-Vatican II sources **are authentic sources**, and **must** be recognised as such before any attempt can be made in evaluating the
genuine contributions made by Vatican II. This council did not
exist and operate in a vacuum: it came from the same Church that
gave us Vatican I and Trent, and wants to be explained in the Light

and Tradition that went before it. If no agreement can be reached on the value of pre-Vatican II Tradition, essential for the explanation of Vatican II, then any divorce from this Tradition will falsify the message of Vatican II.

> (ii) The Bishops and the Magisterium: Am I realistic in stressing what I stress? Do I echo the voice of the Magisterium; or, if not, what is the position?

(iii)

This point does raise one of the more prominent dilemmas of our time. I have never been accused of having been at variance with papal teaching, either before or after Vatican II, or with Vatican II itself, not even in my private correspondence with Priests and Bishops. **Rome** has never laboured under a false interpretation of Vatican II, which is not amazing, really, since Vatican II itself is solidly orthodox. If false teaching is rampant, and if Rome and Vatican II are not the source, then the next in line are the Bishops. I am sure that many Episcopal Conferences have their silent minorities, who will uphold the Truth in their respective dioceses under trying circumstances. Which can only mean that a great many Bishops have allowed the spread of cockle and refused to identify it as such, even if it was sold as wheat to the children of God under their care.

(iii) Bishops and the 'church of darkness'.

It is inevitable that the powers of darkness will ensnare Hierarchies, but **not** unless these Hierarchies allowed themselves to be ensnared. This can only come from an inner rupture. If, as a teacher, I see wrong thinking in a child, and wrong reasoning, followed by wrong actions; I call it wrong. I would not be much of a teacher if I allowed erroneous ideas to develop in the children who are entrusted to my care. If I see the same thing in academics, I still call it wrong. If I see it done by Bishops, I still call it wrong. Must I, now that it is done and being allowed to be done by **Hierarchies**, start to doubt my original beliefs and conclusions and start to call wrong right, and false true, just because of the scale of the evil? If I still call it wrong, out comes the 'trump card' of the Modernists: "Aren't you accusing the Holy Spirit of having abandoned His Church?" Of course I deny that: "No, not all. Bishops who act like that have rather abandoned the Holy Spirit." About Gethsemane it was **not** written: "… and then the Apostles were abandoned by Jesus, Who fled …"; but "… and then the Apostles left Him and fled …". That was then the **whole Hierarchy**, future Pope included. So, a whole Hierarchy abandoning the Holy Father in his efforts to guard the Deposit of Faith is no proof that the Holy Spirit has abandoned His Church. Dying is no sign of abandonment. A dying Church is a Church in love. A Church very much in love with God. A **strong** Church …

The Search For The Modern Synthesis

We are now rapidly approaching the central tension in present-day Catholic thinking. We all agree that it is to be found in the pages of Vatican II. Does it lie in a new emancipation of thought, in the direction of 'modern evolutionary theory' as advocated by Teilhard, and supposedly spread out in the documents of Vatican II; or, if not, what is it?

I think that the uniqueness of modern Catholic thought lies in a totally different direction: in the **dimension** initiated by **Fatima**: in the science, the art, the theology and philosophy of **martyrdom**. Of dying for a cause, while living. Of slowly dying to oneself, day by day, under Communism …

The ingredients are all there …

In the twisted reasoning of the hijackers, the fanaticism of the revolutionaries, the determination of the liberation movement as well as the martyrs for the Faith. It is pathetic to see the inspirations of the great liberation movements of our times bent and twisted to suit enslavement. But one day, under Christ, all these fragments of the grasps of the most noble in our days will be gathered in the one Faith, under the one Shepherd, for the advancement of His Kingdom. And then we will have true ecumenism. **Fatima** is unique because it has captivated so profoundly the **true** greatness of contemporary thought: **martyrdom**. And the freedom and mystique that this Truth carried with it spilled over in Vatican II for the benefit of 'modern man': that pathetic end product of a faked evolution.

This is the 'discipline of the mind' that I have tried to capture and analyse in the pages of my writing, to give heart to the lonely Catholics abandoned by all who were formerly worthy of their trust …

If **Vatican II**, then, shares in the Mystery of the Catholic Church, and the Catholic Church is the Bride of the Lamb of God; may we ask Christ to yield to us sinners, His Secret, for the benefit of those who depend on us for their salvation? On the way we keep and live our Catholic Faith?

The first thing we can say about a mystery is that it is not immediately understood; and the essence of a Supernatural Mystery is that it can only be partly seen and understood in the Supernatural Light of Catholic Faith. The Mystery surrounding Christ is that He has a Life of his own. We see Him live His life on earth: attend to the sick; the poor; the hungry; the sinners. But that is not all there is to Him. There is His Mystical Life: His Life in God; His own, personal relationship with the Father. And of that Life we only get glimpses. The same is true for the Holy Virgin, the Mother of God. We can see Her go about Her business in Nazareth, but that is not all there is to Her. She is the Mystical Rose; the Ark of the Covenant, where She too lives Her life in seclusion in the presence of God. And the great Mystery of the Church, the Bride of the Lamb of God, is that she too shares in the Mystical Union of the Lamb of God; modeling Herself on Her Mother and Proto-type, the Blessed Virgin Mary.

We see the Church administer to the faithful, attending to their every need. But deep down She too lives a Life of Her own, hidden and secluded in the intimate union with Her Spouse, of which we may occasionally get some glimpses. But it is there: alive, active and vibrant. And some of this came out in Vatican II, showing that, while hammering out the pastoral care for the sheep of decades to come, Vatican II shared in the Mystery of the Church; and became an instrument of the Holy Spirit in a more than usual outpouring of the signs of this Life. For, apparently, the hour had come for the Church ...

Enough is known of the Lives of the great Saints to accept that here on earth the Mystical Union with God is lived in the **embrace of suffering**. It is not easily understood why this is, or should be; but the Saints have given us an inkling of how they saw their union with Christ, and Christ's union with God. We become further acquainted with this Reality when we read the rules the founders of the great Orders in the Church have left for the formation of their followers. For the edification and benefit of my readers, I will print in full the famous '11th Rule' of the *Summary of the Constitution*, written by the great mystic St. **Ignatius of Loyola** for the spiritual formation of the Jesuits:

[11] "They must with great diligence observe (in fact they must think highly of it, and consider it of the greatest importance in the sight of the Creator and Our Lord) how much it helps and stimulates towards progress in the spiritual life, to be totally, and not half-heartedly, abhorred by everything the World loves and embraces; and to accept and even desire with all their might whatever Christ Our Lord embraced with such great love. For just as worldly people who follow all that is of this world, with great determination and love and seek honours, a great name and fame here on earth, as the world teaches them; so must they, who walk in the spirit and

seriously follow Christ Our Lord, love and ardently desire all that is totally contrary to this: to be dressed that is with the same dress and to wear the same badges as their Lord, out of love and reverence for Him; even to the extent that, if it could be done without any offense to the Divine Majesty or involve a sin by their neighbour, they would wish to suffer outrages, false testimonies and injustices, and even to be taken as stupid (without on their part giving any cause for that), for the sole reason that they wish to be identified with, and to follow in some way our Creator and Lord, Jesus Christ, and to wear the same dress and insignis as He did. For He wore them first for our greater spiritual profit, and He left us an example, so that we would love to imitate Him in everything and to follow Him, as He is the true road that leads men to Life."

It is obvious, as comes out in his Spiritual Exercises, that St. Ignatius is here thinking of the purple robe of derision, by which Herod dressed Christ and in which he sent Him to Pilate: of the spittle and Blood that Veronica wiped from His adorable face; but even more so of the following sentence in the Gospel of St. John: "Jesus then came out, wearing the crown of thorns and the purple robe", the insignia of a mock king. (Jn. 19:5). According to the great Saints: this is what Love made Christ embrace in the Mystery of His Mystical Life here on earth. It is the same Life that, deep down, His Spouse and Mystical Body: the Church, also wishes to live, according to the testimony of the just quoted 11th Rule.

This Mystery of Christ, this Mystical Life in the Son of God on earth, in His Holy Mother, in His Bride and in the great Saints is the easiest to guard: not only is it hidden and not understood by anyone who does not share in the Supernatural Light of Faith; it is increased every time a persecutor lays his hands on Christ's followers.

If the Holy Catholic Church, foreseeing with the far sightedness of a loving mother the imminent spiritual drought to follow, wished the Vatican Council to bring the Mystery of this Life to the attention of a greater number of her children, then all we have to finally do is to establish:

Did Vatican II stress this whole mystical union between Christ and His Church, and did she recommend it more than usual to Catholics for their daily practice?

1. The Message of Vatican II

(i) The Call to Holiness.

I think that no other Council in the history of the Church has so persistently, and in such a varied way, called Catholics to an unbounded Holiness as has Vatican II. In Chapter V of the *Dogmatic Constitution of the Church*, No. 39, this call to holiness is directly related to the Mystery of the Church.

"The Church, whose Mystery is set forth by this sacred Council, is held, as a matter of Faith, to be unfailingly holy. This is because Christ, the Son of God, loved the Church His Bride, giving Himself up for her so as to sanctify her."

In nearly every one of its sixteen documents, the sacred Council comes back to this question of holiness, great holiness. She gives her approval to the practice that many people in the world follow the Evangelical Counsels "as a striking witness and example" to that holiness. There is to be no bar to the striving for perfection: "they are to follow in Christ's footsteps and be conformed to His image" (we know what He looked like, wearing the purple robe and the crown of thorns: an imitation of Christ, formerly considered to be reserved for Religious, as the 11th Rule of St. Ignatius testifies). (*Lumen Gentium*, 40). She expects this "of all Christians …".

Likewise, the Church expects all the faithful: "to have the same mind of Christ, Who empties Himself, taking the form of a servant, and became obedient unto death" (Phil. 2: 7-8) and for our sake "became poor though He was rich" (2 Cor. 8:9). Since the disciples must always imitate this love and humility of Christ, and bear witness to it, "Mother Church rejoices that She has within Herself many men and women who pursue more closely the Saviour's self-emptying and show it forth more clearly by undertaking poverty with the freedom of God's sons, and renouncing their own will" (*Lumen Gentium*, 42).

After having invited everybody indiscriminately to these highest standards of perfection, the Council never comes down from these lofty heights in the subsequent documents, dealing with individual sections in the Church. The Council has made everybody aware of the great Mystery of the Church in Her intimate life with Her Beloved Spouse, and has extended an invitation to everyone to come and taste a share of that Life and be prepared to pay the price, a very high price …

(ii) Persecutions, which the Church never lacks.

In a dozen or so places in Her documents, the Council reminds us of the ultimate consequences of what it means to be a Christian and a follower of Christ. It is as if She has a premonition 'that Her hour too has finally come, and that, just as Christ had to go through His own Agony, Passion and Death in order to come to the end of Satan's boast, and to wrench the control over the kingdoms of this earth from his grasp, now the Church may be called upon to faithfully follow Her Spouse on the Royal Road to Calvary, in order to come to the end of Teilhard's boast, and loosen his control over the mind of 'modern man'. For there is no escaping it: in several places the Church reminds Her children in the documents of Vatican II "to be prepared to be called upon to shed their blood". And it is apparently fixed in Her Motherly Mind, that there is no better way to bring up this supreme sacrifice of our lives, than to first share more fully in the Mystical Life She shares with Her Spouse. Hence Her insistence that we should seriously consider Her urgent invitations to participate more fully Her own union with Her Spouse.

"For the Catholic Church is by the will of God the teacher of Truth. It is Her duty to proclaim and teach with authority the Truth which is Christ, and, at the same time, to declare and confirm by Her Authority the principles of the Moral Order which spring from human nature itself. In addition, Christians should approach those who are outside wisely, 'in the Holy Spirit, genuine love, truthful speech' (2 Cor. 6: 6-7), and should strive, even to the shedding of their blood, to spread the light of Life with all confidence and apostolic courage'." (*Religious Liberty*, 14).

"Since Jesus, the Son of God, showed His love by laying down His Life for us, no one has greater love than he who lays down his life for Him and for his brothers. Some Christians have been called from the beginning, and will always be called to give this greatest testimony of love to all, especially to persecutors. Martyrdom makes the disciple like his Master, and through it he is conformed to Him by the shedding of blood ... All however must be prepared to confess Christ before men and to follow Him along the way of the Cross amidst the persecutions which the Church never lacks." (*Lumen Gentium*, 42).

"There is an imperative need for the individual Apostolate in those areas where the Church's freedom is seriously hampered. In such difficult circumstances the laity take over as far as possible the work of Priests, jeopardizing their own freedom and sometimes their lives. They teach Christian Doctrine to those around them, train them in a religious way of life and in Catholic attitudes, encouraging them to receive the Sacraments frequently and to cultivate piety, especially Eucharistic piety. The Council renders God most heartfelt thanks that even in our own times He is still raising up laymen with heroic courage in the midst of persecutions. The council embraces them with gratitude and fatherly affection." (*Decree on the Laity*, 17).

From these and similar declarations (*Priests*, 13; *Missions*, 42. e.g.) it is obvious that the Council expects a more than usual training in holiness and perseverance. Therefore, not leaving this to chance, the Sacred Council – as we already saw – brings us face to face with a Model: a Model of Perfection.

(iii) Mary, Mother of the Church.

No need to dwell on the incredible riches the Council has put before us in developing Her Marian doctrine. Sufficient to point out here that the Church has very much the training to great holiness in Mind, when She referred all of us to Mary, the New Eve, the Virgin who was not deceived and the cause of our salvation: the foundations of Marian doctrine and piety which, in other words, were laid down at the time of the Apostles. By letting us draw up great sustenance from the deepest roots of Marian devotion in the Catholic Church, the Council no doubt hoped that the fruits of great holiness and perseverance She found it necessary to cultivate and expect under the guidance of the Holy Spirit, would indeed be forthcoming. And after expounding Her doctrine, the Council could not have left us in better hands: the same hands to which God entrusted His Son.

2. The Servant of Jahweh

That rejection, humiliation, suffering and even death are the outward signs of a great mystical union between a human being and God, was not unbeknown to the Old Testament writers and prophets, although they lacked the model from which they could learn and Whom they could imitate. And even in the New Dispensation, where we have "such a great cloud of witnesses even from the Old Testament", and have the example of Jesus before our very eyes, "we still have to steady our trembling knees", (Hebr. 12, 1 and 12).

So in this we have a 'cloud of witnesses ...'. We also have the example of Our Lord Himself: "Was it not ordained that the Christ should suffer and so enter into His glory?" (Lk. 24:26).

Four passages Our Lord almost certainly drew the attention of His spellbound listeners to must have been the 'Songs of the Servant of Jahweh, in **Isaiah** 42: 1-7; 49: 1-9; 50: 4-9; and especially 52: 13-53: 12. According to the parallelism of St. Paul, we may – within suitable safeguards – apply the main line of thought to the Church: rejected, in order to become "the Light of Nations" (Is. 49:6; Acts. 13:47).

Conclusion

Here then, I think, we have all the ingredients for the <u>new synthesis</u>:

(a) We have an unbroken and immutable Catholic Tradition, the roots of which go deep into the Old Covenant, rejecting everything that cannot show its origin or its credentials if compared to these: which in our days is the fate of evolution.

(b) We are called to a much greater holiness,

(c) We are called to a deep and rich Marian spirituality,

(d) We are called to embrace the world, not in the way Teilhard de Chardin meant it; but in the way Christ did it when He entered His last day on earth.

To make matters worse: the three main roots that would have given stability and nourishment to Catholics in the transition to the post-Conciliar Church:

(i) a sound and cherished knowledge of the living Catholic Tradition in ones' own country,

(ii) devotion to Our Lady of Fatima, and

(iii) the **Philosophia Perennis**, or the Catholic Philosophy of St. **Thomas Aquinas.**

all became discredited or obscured by the ferocious onslaught of the Teilhardian 'church of darkness'.

But one line held ... headed by the Holy Father. And we cannot be surprised that this line consists of Catholics who, steeped in the Traditions of their own country, with a singular devotion to Our Lady of Fatima and with the so necessary 'discipline of the mind', have rejected Teilhardism and its false interpretations of Vatican II; and who are now in a privileged position of 'undoing the knot of Eve of our time', and of passing the Catholic Church wholly intact to the next generation. To these heroes and heroines, youthful and old, I devote my entire opus.

On the Feast Day of Our Lady of Fatima.
October 13, 1979.

About the Author

Frits Albers, Ph. B (1921-2000), was born in Holland and studied under the Jesuits at Nijmegen during the 1940s. He emigrated to Australia in 1951 and travelled extensively within the south-east region of the 'lucky country'. He joined the Department of Education in Victoria and worked as a high school teacher who specialised in mathematics, French and English.

In the early post Vatican II period, he realised that the strange interpretations of the recently concluded Council that were being forced upon Catholics were under pinned by the same philosophy he had been taught in the 1940's by the Jesuits at Nijmegen in the name of St Thomas Aquinas, but which in reality was the systematic Modernism of Pierre Teilhard De Chardin, S.J. Thus, in the early 1970's he began writing articles and books to expose the philosophical root of these errors and aberrations of Teilhard De Chardin, and to defend Catholic Faith, clear thinking, and right philosophy.

www.ingramcontent.com/pod-product-compliance
Lightning Source LLC
Chambersburg PA
CBHW070023100426
42740CB00013B/2578